The Seedbed Daily Text

LISTEN TO HIM

FORTY STEPS ON THE ROAD TO RESURRECTION

Lent

J. D. WALT

Cover and page design by Strange Last Name
Page layout by PerfecType, Nashville, Tennessee

Walt, John David.
  Listen to him : forty steps on the road to resurrection : Lent / J.D. Walt. – Franklin, Tennessee : Seedbed Publishing, ©2018.

    pages ; cm. – (The Seedbed daily text)

    ISBN 9781628246551 (paperback)
    ISBN 9781628246568 (Mobi)
    ISBN 9781628246575 (ePub)
    ISBN 9781628246582 (uPDF)

    1. Lent--Devotional literature. 2. Lent--Prayers and devotions. 3. Lent--Meditations. 4. Spiritual exercises. I. Title. II. Seedbed daily text.

BV85.W337 2018   242.3   2018962539

 Seedbed

SEEDBED PUBLISHING
Franklin, Tennessee
seedbed.com

Contents

How the Daily Text Works

It seems obvious to say, but I write the Daily Text every day. I mostly write it the day before it is scheduled to release online.

Speaking of that, before we go further, I would like to cordially invite you to subscribe and receive the daily e-mail. Visit dailytext.seedbed.com to get started. Check out the weekly fasting challenge while you are there, and also the very active Facebook group.

Eventually, the daily postings become part of a Daily Text discipleship resource. That's what you hold in your hands now.

It's not exactly a Bible study, though the Bible is both the source and subject. You will learn something about the Bible along the way: its history, context, original languages, and authors. My goal is not educational in nature but transformational. I am more interested in our knowing Jesus than I am in our knowing *about* Jesus.

To that end, each reading begins with the definitive inspiration of the Holy Spirit, the ongoing, unfolding text of Scripture. Following this is a short and, hopefully, substantive insight from the text and some aspect of its meaning. For insight to lead to deeper influence, we turn the text into prayer. Finally, influence must run its course toward impact. This is why we ask each other questions. These questions are not designed to elicit information but to crystallize intention.

Discipleship always leads from inspiration to intention and from attention to action.

Using the Daily Text as a Discipleship Curricular Resource for Groups

While Scripture always addresses us personally, it is not written to us individually. The content of Scripture cries out for a community to address. The Daily Text is made for discipleship in community. This resource can work in several different ways. It could be read like a traditional book, a few pages or chapters at a time. Though unadvisable, the readings could be crammed in on the night before the meeting. Keep in mind, the Daily Text is not called the Daily Text for kicks. We believe Scripture is worthy of our most focused and consistent attention. Every day. We all have misses, but let's make every day more than a noble aspiration. Let's make it our covenant with one another.

For Use with Bands

In our judgment, the best and highest use of the Daily Text is made through what we call banded discipleship. A band is a same-gender group of three to five people who read together, pray together, and meet together to help one another grow into the fullness of Jesus Christ in this life. With banded discipleship, the daily readings serve more as a common text for the band and grist for the interpersonal conversation mill between meetings. The band meeting is reserved for the specialized activities of high-bar discipleship.

To learn more about bands and banded discipleship, visit discipleshipbands.com. Be sure to download the free *Guide to Micro-Community Discipleship* or order a supply of the printed booklets online. Also be sure to explore our online platform for bands at app.newroombands.com.

For Use with Classes and Small Groups

The Daily Text has also proven to be a helpful discipleship resource for a variety of small groups, from community groups to Sunday school classes. Here are some suggested guidelines for deploying the Daily Text as a resource for a small group or class setting.

I. Hearing the Text

Invite the group to settle into silence for a period of no less than one and no more than five minutes. Ask an appointed person to keep time and to read the biblical text covering the period of days since the last group meeting. Allow at least one minute of silence following the reading of the text.

II. Responding to the Text

Invite anyone from the group to respond to the reading by answering these prompts: What did you hear? What did you see? What did you otherwise sense from the Lord?

III. Sharing Insights and Implications for Discipleship

Moving in an orderly rotation (or free-for-all), invite people to share insights and implications from the week's readings. What did you find challenging, encouraging, provocative, comforting, invasive, inspiring, corrective, affirming, guiding, or warning? Allow group conversation to proceed at will. Limit to one sharing item per turn, with multiple rounds of discussion.

Note: this resource comes with a free series of online streaming videos for each week's group meeting. In them, I share a seven- to ten-minute reflection on some aspect of the Scripture readings from the prior week. Some groups like to play the video at the beginning of this group sharing time as a way of kicking off the conversation.

IV. Shaping Intentions for Prayer

Invite each person in the group to share a single discipleship intention for the week ahead. It is helpful if the intention can also be framed as a question the group can use to check in from the prior week. At each person's turn, he or she is invited to share how their intention went during the previous week. The class or group can open and close their meeting according to their established patterns.

On the Season of Lent

The season of Lent is an ancient practice of the church, traditionally engaged to prepare men and women for baptism on the day of Easter. The word comes from an old English word, *lencten*, which means, "spring," and connects with the notion of lengthening days. One of the key practices of Lent is fasting. Sundays, however, are always feast days. Properly speaking, the six Sundays of Lent are not counted in the forty days. Lent begins on Ash Wednesday and continues through Holy Saturday. Ash Wednesday is a preparatory rite of passage, a solemn occasion for repentance and faith; it is ideal for focusing attention and clarifying intention.

This Daily Text series begins with the Tuesday preceding Ash Wednesday. On Shrove Tuesday (a.k.a. Fat Tuesday), the day before Ash Wednesday, we will gather on the Mount of Transfiguration. Ash Wednesday begins our journey of descent to the cross. Our journey runs the route from Luke 9:18 through 24:8. While the daily reflections focus on the Scripture text, it is imperative to understand that the Daily Text is not intended to be centered around my writings but on the Word of God. Please do not skip or even skim the reading of the Scripture text. I encourage you to read it aloud as much as possible so your ears can hear it. Remember, faith comes by hearing. An audio version of the Daily Text can be found at seedbed.com/dailytext.

Each day's reading and reflection leads to a prayer and a question. The prayer will remain consistent for the whole way. Please read the introduction to grasp the significance of the daily prayer and for guidance on engaging it. The question is meant for personal reflection and discussion with others. The Daily Text has become grist for the mill in many discipleship settings and contexts—from Sunday school classes and community groups to discipleship bands and mentoring circles. Also available with this series are additional resources to enable church-wide engagement, including guidance for a preaching series and helps for utilizing the resource in classes and groups. Visit Seedbed.com to learn more.

This resource is also available on our Discipleship Bands App, which can be downloaded from the various app stores online. Visit discipleshipbands.com to learn more. In short, a discipleship band is a group of three to five men or women who read together, pray together, and meet together to become the love of God for one another and the world. When it comes to sustained deep growth in life and faith, discipleship bands consistently deliver.

The Seedbed Daily Text is a growing global fellowship of sowers for a great awakening. It can be accessed online at seedbed.com/dailytext or subscribed to via a daily e-mail. It can be listened to via a link on the daily post and e-mail, through the iTunes Podcast site, and by means of an Amazon Echo device. We also have a flourishing Facebook group for those who enjoy that format.

Introduction
The Journey Starts Here

I don't know why I had the book or how it came into my possession. I have no idea what inspired me to read it in the throes of the insanity that are law school final exams. But read it I did. Through this lesser-known, puzzling novel of a reclusive, enigmatic author, the Spirit of God awakened me to the Son of God who awakened me to the love of God, all of which I knew much about and yet through a glass dimly— still at a level I might have understood property law or torts.

You must be wondering about this book. Despite its triggered landmine explosion in my life, I'm not recommending it, other than to name it as one of those mysterious divine providences whereby, in the words of a Trappist monk, "God gets us where he wants us, no matter the machinations." The author was J. D. Salinger, whose most famous book, *The Catcher in the Rye*, still eludes my reading. The book—*Franny and Zooey*—released in 1961, combined two short stories about a sister and brother, respectively, earlier published by Salinger in *The New Yorker* in 1955 and 1957.

The book tells the story of Franny, a college student in search of purpose, tossed by the waves of the meaninglessness of modern academia and on the brink of emotional breakdown. On a date with her boyfriend, she recounts a mysterious book that had come into her possession, *The Way of a Pilgrim*, and its strange impact on her life, introducing her to a mantra of sorts known as the "Jesus Prayer."

And what, you ask, is the Jesus Prayer? Twelve insanely economical, unutterably comprehensive words: "Lord Jesus Christ, Son of God, have mercy on me, a sinner."

Here's Franny in her own words on the point of the prayer:

> The Jesus Prayer has one aim, and one aim *only*. To endow the person who says it with Christ-consciousness. *Not* to set up some little cozy, holier-than-thou trysting place with some sticky, adorable divine *personage* who'll take you in his arms and relieve you of all your duties and make all your nasty *weltschmerzen* and Professor Tuppers go away and never come back. And by God, if you have intelligence enough to see that—and you *do*—and yet you refuse to see it, then you're misusing the prayer, you're using it to ask for a world full of dolls and saints and no Professor Tuppers.[1]

Searching for purpose and tossed to and fro by the waves of a late adolescent crisis of meaning and purpose, I adopted not only the prayer but Franny's way of praying it. It took on a kind of holy obsession for me. I prayed it as my feet hit the floor in the morning. I prayed it as I brushed my teeth. I prayed it at meals. I prayed it in class.

---

1 J. D. Salinger, *Franny and Zooey* (1955; repr., New York: Bantam Books, 1981), 172.

Lord Jesus Christ, Son of God, have mercy on me, a sinner.

Like most other Christians I had ever known, I knew Jesus as Savior in a transactional way. I am not sure I knew Jesus as Lord until I began to address him as such with such constancy. I assented to the inevitable fact of my being a sinner, much like a box one would check for a preexisting condition (like say a heart murmur, on a medical form). While I had a clear concept of mercy, I had no conception of my actual need for it.

Though I was praying the prayer consistently, I did not begin praying unceasingly until the prayer connected with my walking. I began to pray the prayer as I moved about the world, each word of it in cadence with the next step. Walking here, walking there, upstairs, downstairs, every step: *Lord Jesus Christ, Son of God, have mercy on me, a sinner.*

Something about the rudimentary nature of steps—all at once conscious and unconscious, intentional yet automatic, labored yet effortless—took me inside of the prayer. As the words of my mouth connected with the steps of my feet, the prayer began to groove a well-worn path through the overgrown underbrush of my soul.

Epiphanies abounded. I began to discover my sin as a reality far deeper than my sins. It was not my sins that made me a sinner. I was born this way. I am not a sinner because I sin. No, I sin because I am a sinner. My problem was not at the level of bad behavior but broken identity. I needed mercy not because of anything I had done but because of who I was. Who was I? As a sinner, my identity could be summed up in one word: a slave. My need for mercy did not rise and fall based on my behavior but was constant and totalizing. This led me to the awakening discovery that Jesus' mercy was more than something he had done. It was his identity. Jesus not only *had* mercy for me, but he was mercy *to* me.

Then the miracle happened. In owning my core identity as a slave, a sinner, and a broken image-bearer of God, Jesus gave me a new identity. He made me a beloved son. With that, my Jesus prayer grew.

Lord Jesus Christ, Son of God, have mercy on me, a son.

I didn't leave behind the first prayer, as though I somehow ceased to be a sinner. I simply added the second.

Why do we need mercy to be sons and daughters? It's one thing to be the grateful recipient of a pardon, but surely there must be more to bearing the image of the triune God than life as a pardoned criminal or even a freed slave. While those are tremendous gifts of grace, they do not begin to touch the enormity of our inheritance. We are the children of God, the sons and daughters of a perfect Father, which makes us the coheirs with the Son of God. On this point, Scripture could not be more clear. Check it out:

> For you did not receive the spirit of slavery to fall back into fear, but you have received the Spirit of adoption as sons, by whom we cry, "Abba! Father!" The Spirit himself bears witness with our spirit that we are children of God, and if children, then heirs—heirs of God and fellow heirs with Christ, provided we suffer with

him in order that we may also be glorified with him.
(Rom. 8:15–17 ESV)

I needed the mercy of forgiveness to pardon my sin and to rescue me from slavery. I needed a new kind of mercy to truly claim my identity and inheritance as a son. This would take the mercy of faith. Why faith? I had read it a thousand times. I was a child of God. I believed it at some level. I sang the songs. Despite all that, this truth had not taken up residence in my deepest self. I think I believed God loved me because he had to love me. I needed to believe this in a much deeper way. I needed to know it in my bones. And so I stepped.

Lord Jesus Christ, Son of God, have mercy on me, a sinner.
Lord Jesus Christ, Son of God, have mercy on me, a son.

Then the miracle happened. In owning my core identity as a son, a beloved child of an adoring Father, I began to rest in who I most deeply was—my true self. He didn't love me for anything I had done or in spite of my failures. He loved me because I belonged to him. And I began to love him because he belonged to me.

I needed the mercy of faith because this whole concept of a gifted identity was stripping away my old slavish system of self-worth. All of my perceived value, which was built around all the ways I performed and pleased my way to the top, had to go so something new and gloriously devastating could rise up in its place. The mercy of faith gave rise to the mercy of freedom as I claimed the newfound gift of an ancient baptism.

In the days of Lent long ago, I learned to eat the blessed word of my own baptism of belovedness: "John David, you are my son, my beloved, with you I am well pleased." Just as Jesus received these words prior to any performance, so would I receive them. Just as Jesus would thwart the temptation to prove his identity by turning stones into bread, so would I—by the saving provision of the Word of God spoken in the sustaining power of the Spirit of God. The mercy of sonship and daughterhood is not a static state, but a dynamic, growing reality which must be fed daily by the bread-like manna of Word and Spirit.

Lord Jesus Christ, Son of God, have mercy on me, a sinner.
Lord Jesus Christ, Son of God, have mercy on me, a son.

As the mercy of forgiveness became faith and the mercy of faith became freedom, I began to discover yet another new mercy—the mercy of fullness. It gave rise to the third and what I believe to be final Jesus prayer.

Lord Jesus Christ, Son of God, have mercy on me, a saint.

I began to discover the power of the love of God. If I could be loved deeply (simply because of who I was), I could love others deeply (simply because of who they were). Carefully consider Paul's prayer from his letter to the Ephesians:

> that according to the riches of his glory he may grant you to be strengthened with power through his Spirit in your inner being, so that Christ may dwell in your hearts through faith—that you, being rooted and

grounded in love, may have strength to comprehend with all the saints what is the breadth and length and height and depth, and to know the love of Christ that surpasses knowledge, that you may be filled with all the fullness of God. (3:16–19 ESV)

The word *saint* means "a holy one." A saint is a person who is "filled to the measure of all the fullness of God" (Eph. 3:19). According to Scripture, the fullness of God is the love of God in Jesus Christ, which turns out to be the power of God.

Mercy is the soul's oxygen. The more desperately we breathe it, the more deeply we become it. In this way, the holy love of God is both our identity and our vocation in the world.

Lord Jesus Christ, Son of God, have mercy on me, a sinner.
Lord Jesus Christ, Son of God, have mercy on me, a
   son/daughter.
Lord Jesus Christ, Son of God, have mercy on me, a saint.

From sinners and slaves to sons and daughters and from sons and daughters to saints of God—this is the path of descent on the way of the cross. Progress moves by way of forgiveness to faith to freedom to fullness. To be clear, it is not a neat and tidy journey. It will be occasioned by great struggle, often by fits and starts and through both crisis and process. It will be gloriously hard and profoundly good.

God gets us where he wants us by way of our walk with him. Our walk with him is comprised by our everyday steps. This is not a step-by-step follow-the-directions kind of process;

rather it is a following Jesus step-by-step as he leads us. I commend these prayers to you through the days of Lent and beyond. To this day, I pray them every day, multiple times a day. They are not magical incantations, but they will become miraculous interventions. Give them time and space. Give them your breath and your steps. Thirty-six words. Thirty-six steps. But this book is called *Listen to Him: Forty Steps on the Road to Resurrection*. Here are four more word steps for the road: Father, Son, Holy Spirit!

And a bonus word: Amen!

Shrove Tuesday

Fat Tuesday on Transfiguration Mountain

LUKE 9:28–36 | About eight days after Jesus said this, he took Peter, John and James with him and went up onto a mountain to pray. As he was praying, the appearance of his face changed, and his clothes became as bright as a flash of lightning. Two men, Moses and Elijah, appeared in glorious splendor, talking with Jesus. They spoke about his departure, which he was about to bring to fulfillment at Jerusalem. Peter and his companions were very sleepy, but when they became fully awake, they saw his glory and the two men standing with him. As the men were leaving Jesus, Peter said to him, "Master, it is good for us to be here. Let us put up three shelters—one for you, one for Moses and one for Elijah." (He did not know what he was saying.)

While he was speaking, a cloud appeared and covered them, and they were afraid as they entered the cloud. A voice came from the cloud, saying, "This is my Son, whom I have chosen; listen to him." When the voice had spoken, they found that Jesus was alone. The disciples kept this to themselves and did not tell anyone at that time what they had seen.

Consider This

We are here—Transfiguration Mountain.

Moses, Elijah, Jesus, Peter, James, and John.

This is the conference of the counsel of the kingdom of God. Moses represents the Law. Elijah represents the Prophets. Rather than representing the gospel, Jesus is the gospel in whom the Law and the Prophets are not only fulfilled but extended into all eternity. Then there are the apostles who will be the church. They represent us. The Law, the Prophets, and the gospel come face-to-face with the Rock and the sons of thunder—the future church.

Jesus, God's Messiah, miraculously unites not only divinity and humanity, but heaven and earth and even the past and the future. In this instance, the representatives of the past are brought into the presence of the representatives of the future and all for the purpose of together beholding the glory of God in the face of Jesus Christ, who was and is and is to come! Everything, literally everything, comes together and coheres and transforms, no, transfigures in him. Transformation is to transfiguration as resuscitation is to resurrection.

As he was praying, the appearance of his face changed, and his clothes became as bright as a flash of lightning.

This is not a dream or a vision or some otherwise ethereal cathartic experience. This, my friends, is the tangible revelation and manifestation of ultimate reality.

> He is the image of the invisible God, the firstborn of all creation. For by him all things were created, in

heaven and on earth, visible and invisible, whether thrones or dominions or rulers or authorities—all things were created through him and for him. And he is before all things, and in him all things hold together. (Col. 1:15–17 ESV)

Remember what Jesus told the disciples? "Truly, I say to you, there are some standing here who will not taste death until they see the kingdom of God" (Mark 9:1 ESV).

Isn't that what Paul was saying?

I tell you this, brothers: flesh and blood cannot inherit the kingdom of God, nor does the perishable inherit the imperishable. Behold! I tell you a mystery. We shall not all sleep, but we shall all be changed, in a moment, in the twinkling of an eye, at the last trumpet. For the trumpet will sound, and the dead will be raised imperishable, and we shall be changed. For this perishable body must put on the imperishable, and this mortal body must put on immortality. When the perishable puts on the imperishable, and the mortal puts on immortality, then shall come to pass the saying that is written: "Death is swallowed up in victory." (1 Cor. 15:50–54 ESV)

On this mountain, the paper-thin veil between heaven and earth is pulled back and we behold eternity as a snapshot in time.

When the kingdom finally comes in all its glory, this is what we will see: Abraham and Sarah, Isaac and Rebekah,

Jacob and Joseph, Moses and Ruth and Samuel and David and Elijah and Mary and Peter and James and John and Lydia and Dorcas and Paul and Barnabas and Perpetua and Polycarp and your grandparents and mine and those loved ones in the Lord who succumbed to cancer and tragedy and the children that left us too soon. Together, we will all be transfigured. "Just as we have borne the image of the man of dust, we shall also bear the image of the man of heaven" (1 Cor. 15:49 ESV).

And at the center of it all we will behold the risen Son of God, the one who not only tasted death but who, as Isaiah prophesied, "will swallow up death forever" (25:8 ESV).

Just when the disciples thought the kingdom had come, and they should make camp, the conference was over. This would prove to be the turning point, the hinge on which the door to the gospel would swing open. From this mountaintop transfiguration high, Jesus will lead us to the lowest place, where the Son of Man will be disfigured on the cross.

That's why Transfiguration Mountain is all at once the best and worst place on the planet to get ready for Ash Wednesday. Ash Wednesday opens the doorway to descent, the place where the truth of our mortality is met with the promise of eternity. From dust you have come and to dust you will return. Repent and believe the gospel. If transfiguration is the destination, transformation shall be the journey.

We are headed to Jerusalem now. The cross before us, the world behind us, no turning back; no turning back.

One more thing . . . I didn't mention it, but we received a massive word from God on Transfiguration Mountain.

"This is my Son, my Chosen One; listen to him!" (Luke 9:35 ESV).

That will be our agenda for these next forty days as we make our way down the mountain and on to Jerusalem. Luke, our skillful guide, will lead the way ahead. We will reconvene and regroup tomorrow at the foot of the mountain.

The Prayer

Lord Jesus Christ, Son of God, have mercy on me, a sinner.
Lord Jesus Christ, Son of God, have mercy on me, a
*   son/daughter.*
Lord Jesus Christ, Son of God, have mercy on me, a saint.

The Question

What does the phrase "Repent and believe the gospel" mean to you at this moment in your life?

Ash Wednesday—Don't Be Afraid to Ask 1

LUKE 9:37–45 | The next day, when they came down from the mountain, a large crowd met him. A man in the crowd called out, "Teacher, I beg you to look at my son, for he is my only child. A spirit seizes him and he suddenly screams; it throws him into convulsions so that he foams at the mouth. It scarcely ever leaves him and is destroying him. I begged your disciples to drive it out, but they could not."

"You unbelieving and perverse generation," Jesus replied, "how long shall I stay with you and put up with you? Bring your son here."

Even while the boy was coming, the demon threw him to the ground in a convulsion. But Jesus rebuked the impure spirit, healed the boy and gave him back to his father. And they were all amazed at the greatness of God.

While everyone was marveling at all that Jesus did, he said to his disciples, "Listen carefully to what I am about to tell you: The Son of Man is going to be delivered into the hands of men." But they did not understand what this meant. It was hidden from them, so that they did not grasp it, and they were afraid to ask him about it.

Consider This

But they did not understand what this meant. It was hidden from them, so that they did not grasp it, and they were afraid to ask him about it.

Can we resolve something here at the outset of this journey to the cross? The greatest hindrance to growing in our understanding of life, faith, Jesus, the world, and the world to come is our present understanding of life, faith, Jesus, the world, and the world to come. It's hard to learn what we think we already know. And that may be our greatest problem: we don't know what we don't know. Know what I mean?

In other words, the more we grow the more difficult growth becomes and the more likely we are to stall out, plateau, and get stuck or arrested in development.

So what's the remedy for this condition? Sometimes it takes a desert to bring us to desperation, which can lead us to humility, making way for the kind of learning that leads to breakthrough growth. The word *disciple* comes from the Greek word *mathetes*, which means, "learner." A disciple is not one who learns by mastering information; rather a disciple is one who learns by submitting to a master. Here's how Jesus describes it:

> "Take my yoke upon you, and learn from me, for I am gentle and lowly in heart, and you will find rest for your souls. For my yoke is easy, and my burden is light." (Matt. 11:29–30 ESV)

This is a perfect invitation to a Holy Lent. Lent invites us to a desert of deepening for the sake of divine love. Lent is not about fasting, though fasting is a key path toward deepening. Lent is not about becoming more disciplined, though discipline comes from the root word, *disciple*. Lent is not about developing an Instagram-oriented designer spirituality so others can #checkoutmyperfectlife. If ever there were a season for #nofilter and no selfies, it is Lent.

Lent opens a time for getting in touch with the holy discontent that comes from having too much of that which does not ultimately matter and too little of that which actually does. Lent unfolds a path allowing holy discontent to lead us into a brokenness before God (whether that be a real-messed-up-ness or a not-quite-right-ness or a somewhere-in-between-ness). Lent extends the invitation to let our brokenness before God lead us to a deeper surrender and truer submission to Jesus. And the outcome? Finally, through this qualitatively different kind of surrender, Lent reveals all the human possibilities of participating in the divine nature, whereby we may escape the corruption that is in the world and live extravagantly generous lives in the embrace of holy love.

There's a way to avoid this outcome: *But they did not understand what this meant. It was hidden from them, so that they did not grasp it, and they were afraid to ask him about it.*

So what was it they failed to understand? *The Son of Man is going to be delivered into the hands of men.*

Of course we get this. It's obvious. We learned it a long time ago. This is basic Christianity 101. Remember how Jesus prefaced this critically important statement? *"Listen carefully to what I am about to tell you."*

Okay, so I will go first. Jesus, as sure as I think that I understand what you said here, I am confident that I don't fully get it. I may not even get it a little bit. I want to ask you to instruct me and lead me deeper into the meaning of your life and death and resurrection. I've been in church all my life, and I have the perfect attendance pins to prove it. I've been to seminary and even work for one. I write books about you. But I confess that what I understand causes me to love you and to want to understand more, and I know that understanding more will cause me to love you more which will lead me to love others more. I'm listening, Jesus.

The Prayer

Lord Jesus Christ, Son of God, have mercy on me, a sinner.
Lord Jesus Christ, Son of God, have mercy on me, a
*   son/daughter.*
Lord Jesus Christ, Son of God, have mercy on me, a saint.

The Question

Do the words *holy discontent* ring a bell or strike a chord in your soul? How would you describe your present state of stuckness, or what might be the growing edge of transformation in your life?

Acknowledge That God's Ways Are Perfect 2

LUKE 9:46–50 | An argument started among the disciples as to which of them would be the greatest. Jesus, knowing their thoughts, took a little child and had him stand beside him. Then he said to them, "Whoever welcomes this little child in my name welcomes me; and whoever welcomes me welcomes the one who sent me. For it is the one who is least among you all who is the greatest."

"Master," said John, "we saw someone driving out demons in your name and we tried to stop him, because he is not one of us."

"Do not stop him," Jesus said, "for whoever is not against you is for you."

Consider This

Jesus really knows how to end an argument.

Do you remember that time when the prophet Isaiah wrote this?

> For my thoughts are not your thoughts,
>> neither are your ways my ways, declares the LORD.
> For as the heavens are higher than the earth,
>> so are my ways higher than your ways
>> and my thoughts than your thoughts.
>> (Isa. 55:8–9 ESV)

Well, this thing going on in today's text is what that is all about.

The ways of God are not only categorically but catastrophically different than our ways.

It's easy to look at today's text and dismiss it as an absurd example that we can't imagine ever being a part of (i.e., having an argument with someone about who is greater) . . . until we reflect on the unquenchable quest of just about every one of us to be number one at something. It's always amusing when the worst team in the league manages to upset a better team and, all of a sudden, all their fans are pompously pointing their index fingers into the air at the TV cameras with the redonkulous claim that they are number one! Whether we can bring ourselves to admit it or not, this quest to be the greatest is in every last one of us.

So what's the alternative? Should we just not care? Should we be complacent? Should we eschew winning and competing to be number one? That's another one of our big problems— to jump to the other extreme, to assume that the opposite of something is always the same thing as the antithesis.

If we have any hope of ever getting the higher thoughts and ways of God (which according to Isaiah, could not possibly be more different than ours), we are going to have to come to grips with this.

In response to the disciples' urinating contest, Jesus says about the most absurd thing imaginable to first-century sensibilities. He gets a child and presents her to the disciples, saying, *"Whoever welcomes this little child in my name welcomes me; and whoever welcomes me welcomes the one who sent me. For it is the one who is least among you all who is the greatest."*

Translation: "For my thoughts are not your thoughts, neither are your ways my ways."

It's hard for us to imagine the perceived worthlessness of a child in the first-century context. A child had a status quotient of less than zero. They were seen as property that had essentially little to no value. The cumulative impact of these words alone on the comparative worth of children today is virtually inestimable. There just weren't any helicopter parents to speak of in those days.

It's mind-blowing. It's the kind of thing you would only take seriously if God said it. And that's pretty much what happened. So back to that "opposite isn't always the antithesis" thought. In my mind, the opposite of the greatest would be the worst. I think Jesus makes the assertion that the antithesis of the greatest is the most humble. When Jesus speaks of becoming like a child in order to inherit the kingdom of God, he is not saying (as we are wont to think) to become playful and whimsical and carefree in the world. That would be to impose a twenty-first-century meaning on a first-century reality. Jesus is talking about becoming humble. He is talking about not considering our status, or that of anyone else, to be the measure of one's worth.

After all, he's the one, "who, though he was in the form of God, did not count equality with God a thing to be grasped, but emptied himself" (Phil. 2:6–7 ESV).

It means the followers of Jesus don't measure themselves or anyone else like the world measures them. If true greatness is ascribed to the least among us, then in order to be great we must understand ourselves as on the level with the least. In order to do this, we must see ourselves and others from another perspective entirely—the perspective of God. God sees the exact same fundamental worth in every single human being.

If I am to love others as I love myself, and my regard for myself is founded on the ways I have managed to distinguish myself (or failed to distinguish myself) from everyone else, then I will love others to the extent that they have also distinguished themselves. And to the extent they have not, I will not value them. But if my regard for myself is founded solely on the value accorded to me by the love of God, then I will love others on the basis of the very same value accorded to them by the love of God. This approach actually destroys the world's value system of least and greatest, and isn't that what someone who says of an apparently worthless person (i.e., a first-century child) that they are the greatest, is essentially saying?

This approach, taken to its logical conclusion, ends with the God-given grace to genuinely love the poor rather than just pity them by helping them out with our spare change. Jesus will later say, "As you have done unto the least of these my brethren, you have done it also to me" (see Matthew 25:40). It's only by the mercy of God that we will finally understand that no matter how different we are from one another and how vast the distance may be between our social status, we have the exact same value. This is the economy of grace. It's what makes grace amazing. It's why grace is the remedy to everything that's wrong with the world. It's the only remedy. Everything else is just a temporary fix, a work-around, a Band-Aid.

This is the extraordinary change that God works in the human heart over a long period of time. It's why salvation can't be reduced to a transaction. Salvation is the lifelong process of conversion, of change from one degree of glory to the next. It comes from beholding Jesus, listening to him, and doing what he says. That never fails.

The Prayer

Lord Jesus Christ, Son of God, have mercy on me, a sinner.
Lord Jesus Christ, Son of God, have mercy on me, a son/daughter.
Lord Jesus Christ, Son of God, have mercy on me, a saint.

The Question

How is your own sense of worth tied up with your accomplishments or social status or lack thereof? Have you realized that your own system of self-worth is the way you treat others? What are the implications of this belief?

3 Take the Long View

LUKE 9:51–62 | As the time approached for him to be taken up to heaven, Jesus resolutely set out for Jerusalem. And he sent messengers on ahead, who went into a Samaritan village to get things ready for him; but the people there did not welcome him, because he was heading for Jerusalem. When the disciples James and John saw this, they asked, "Lord, do you want us to call fire down from heaven to destroy them?" But Jesus turned and rebuked them. Then he and his disciples went to another village.

As they were walking along the road, a man said to him, "I will follow you wherever you go."

Jesus replied, "Foxes have dens and birds have nests, but the Son of Man has no place to lay his head."

He said to another man, "Follow me."

But he replied, "Lord, first let me go and bury my father."

Jesus said to him, "Let the dead bury their own dead, but you go and proclaim the kingdom of God."

Still another said, "I will follow you, Lord; but first let me go back and say goodbye to my family."

Jesus replied, "No one who puts a hand to the plow and looks back is fit for service in the kingdom of God."

Consider This

There's a lot we could delve into today, including Samaritan hospitality, apostolic napalm, the homelessness of God, and such. As I worked through today's text, one word stands out to me and I think it captures not only today's passage, but one of the key essences of following Jesus and especially *listening to him*.

If you'd like, take a minute and read back through the text and see what one word stands out to you as capturing today's passage and clarifying a key dynamic of discipleship. (Okay, I'm going to get a second cup of coffee while you do that.)

So what did you come up with? Here's my answer: *resolutely*.

As the time approached for him to be taken up to heaven, Jesus resolutely set out for Jerusalem.

First, note the prefatory words here.

Remember, there are no superfluous words in the Word of God. Every single word matters. They all hold infinite revelation—not in a magical way and certainly not in some relativistic way, but in a meaningful way. I cannot over-stress the need for the people of God (i.e., the church) to raise the bar on our engagement with the Word of God. Our aim is not to master the text but to be mastered by the text. Because I know that's why you read the Daily Text, that's why I write it.

As the time approached for him to be taken up to heaven . . .

Our relationship with Jesus, our discipleship, must be framed in terms of the big picture. Note, Luke doesn't say, "As the time approached for him to be betrayed, handed over to the religious authorities, mocked and beaten by Roman soldiers, sentenced by a middle manager of Caesar, nailed to a cross, and buried in a tomb." No, Luke takes the long view, he sees past the suffering, even beyond the resurrection and all the way to the enthronement of Jesus at the right hand of the Father.

Clearly Jesus knew this unspeakable suffering was coming, and he spoke explicitly about it to his disciples, but he always held a bigger picture. He took the long view. Isn't that what the writer of Hebrews was getting at when he said, "For the joy that was set before him he endured the cross, despising the shame, and is seated at the right hand of the throne of God" (12:2 ESV).

The followers of Jesus take the long view. This doesn't mean some kind of easy escapism or a defeated resignation to simply endure the hardships ahead. It doesn't mean delaying life until after death. It's not a "Things are going to get better, someday," approach. It's not a "Grit your teeth and bear it" mentality.

The soundtrack for the followers of Jesus is not, "Some sweet morning when this life is over, I'll fly away." The soundtrack for discipleship is more like, "We will rock you!" and "We are the champions!" albeit in a humble sort of way. I am indebted to the British theologian Jeremy Begbie for this insight from one of his lectures where he said, "Christians do not hope 'in' the future. We hope 'from' the future." In other words, we aren't hoping everything is going to turn out okay in the end. We live as those who have already won. The future is a settled matter. Because of Jesus, the future is as fixed as the sun. Our hope is not rooted in our hopefulness. It is securely anchored in the settled future. We hope *from* the future.

Jesus resolutely set out for Jerusalem.

Back to our word of the day: *resolutely*. Resoluteness in the present comes from confidence in the future. Resoluteness, in the way of Jesus, is not about a "you can do whatever you set your mind to," self-confident, doggedly determined, boot-strapping-your-way, "Little Engine That Could" work ethic. Resoluteness, in the way of Jesus, comes from an

J. D. WALT

umbilical-like, life-support relationship with Jesus because he not only holds our future, he is our future. It's why the apostolic writers wrote things like,

> Who shall separate us from the love of Christ? Shall tribulation, or distress, or persecution, or famine, or nakedness, or danger, or sword? As it is written,
>
>> "For your sake we are being killed all the day long; we are regarded as sheep to be slaughtered."
>
> No, in all these things we are more than conquerors through him who loved us. For I am sure that neither death nor life, neither angels nor rulers, neither things present nor things to come, nor powers, nor height nor depth, nor anything else in all creation, will be able to separate us from the love of God in Christ Jesus our Lord. (Rom. 8:35–39 ESV)
>
> Therefore, since we are surrounded by so great a cloud of witnesses, let us also lay aside every weight, and sin which clings so closely, and let us run with endurance the race that is set before us, looking to Jesus, the founder and perfecter of our faith. (Heb. 12:1–2 ESV)

Somebody stop me! No matter what obstacle or hardship or disease or persecution or difficult future you are facing today or cross you may be bearing tomorrow . . . don't be afraid of it . . . don't resign yourself to it . . . don't try to be strong and triumphalistic about it . . . instead, invite the Holy Spirit to fill you with a "joy set before us" unshakable confidence in the future and to empower you in your inner being with the very resoluteness of Jesus to be alive with a life beyond your own in the face of it. This is what he does.

The Prayer
Lord Jesus Christ, Son of God, have mercy on me, a sinner.
Lord Jesus Christ, Son of God, have mercy on me, a son/daughter.
Lord Jesus Christ, Son of God, have mercy on me, a saint.

The Question
How do you understand the difference between hoping *in* the future and hoping *from* the future? What does this have to do with your present?

Listen with Your Ears 4

LUKE 10:1–16 | After this the Lord appointed seventy-two others and sent them two by two ahead of him to every town and place where he was about to go. He told them, "The harvest is plentiful, but the workers are few. Ask the Lord of the harvest, therefore, to send out workers into his harvest field. Go! I am sending you out like lambs among wolves. Do not take a purse or bag or sandals; and do not greet anyone on the road.

"When you enter a house, first say, 'Peace to this house.' If someone who promotes peace is there, your peace will rest on them; if not, it will return to you. Stay there, eating and drinking whatever they give you, for the worker deserves his wages. Do not move around from house to house.

"When you enter a town and are welcomed, eat what is offered to you. Heal the sick who are there and tell them, 'The kingdom of God has come near to you.' But when you enter a town and are not welcomed, go into its streets and say, 'Even the dust of your town we wipe from our feet as a warning to you. Yet be sure of this: The kingdom of God has come near.' I tell you, it will be more bearable on that day for Sodom than for that town.

"Woe to you, Chorazin! Woe to you, Bethsaida! For if the miracles that were performed in you had been performed in Tyre and Sidon, they would have repented long ago, sitting in sackcloth and ashes. But it will be more bearable for Tyre and Sidon at the judgment than for you. And you, Capernaum, will you be lifted to the heavens? No, you will go down to Hades.

"Whoever listens to you listens to me; whoever rejects you rejects me; but whoever rejects me rejects him who sent me."

Consider This

Let's begin today with the last verse in the daily text.

Whoever listens to you listens to me; whoever rejects you rejects me; but whoever rejects me rejects him who sent me.

Consider that Jesus is speaking this word directly to you or to me. "[Insert your name], whoever listens to you listens to me; whoever rejects you rejects me."

Humor me, and speak that sentence aloud with your name inserted as though Jesus were speaking it directly to you. Remember what the voice of God spoke on the top of Transfiguration Mountain? Of course you remember, but in case not, he said, "This is my Son, whom I have chosen; listen to him."

I think we must take that word quite literally. It's hard to listen if no one is actually speaking. I don't know about you, but I don't think I actually listen when I read. In order to listen to something or someone, I must "hear" them. Right? When I read, I think, process, understand (sometimes), and so forth, but I don't listen, because I don't hear. The Word of God was not written primarily to be read, but to be heard. As the Scriptures say, "Faith comes from hearing" (Rom. 10:17). I don't think it's possible to listen without hearing.

In light of this, I want to issue a challenge for us on this journey to the cross. Whenever Jesus speaks in the text, speak it aloud. It will be a good step in our effort to "listen to him."

Whoever listens to you [insert your name] listens to me; whoever rejects you [insert your name] rejects me; but whoever rejects me rejects him who sent me.

Did you feel the gravity of that sentence? It's astonishing. Jesus is effectively making you his agent. In other words, you represent Jesus. You speak for him. Listening to you is the same thing as listening to him.

Rather than giving you more to read, I'm going to stop there. I want to ask you to give your full attention to this claim. Is this true? If so, what are the implications? As a final step, I'd like to ask you to write the bolded sentence (including your name) somewhere you can see it and rehearse it (aloud) each day on this journey to the cross. Please.

For my money, and I've never thought or articulated it as such, but this is the singular point of discipleship-serving as the agent of Jesus. Am I missing something?

The Prayer

Lord Jesus Christ, Son of God, have mercy on me, a sinner.
Lord Jesus Christ, Son of God, have mercy on me, a
*   son/daughter.*
Lord Jesus Christ, Son of God, have mercy on me, a saint.

The Question

If you really believed this about being Jesus' agent, what difference would it make in your life? Be practical with your answer.

First Sunday of Lent

Learn Jesus' Most Exuberant Prayer

LUKE 10:17–24 | The seventy-two returned with joy and said, "Lord, even the demons submit to us in your name."

He replied, "I saw Satan fall like lightning from heaven. I have given you authority to trample on snakes and scorpions and to overcome all the power of the enemy; nothing will harm you. However, do not rejoice that the spirits submit to you, but rejoice that your names are written in heaven."

At that time Jesus, full of joy through the Holy Spirit, said, "I praise you, Father, Lord of heaven and earth, because you have hidden these things from the wise and learned, and revealed them to little children. Yes, Father, for this is what you were pleased to do.

"All things have been committed to me by my Father. No one knows who the Son is except the Father, and no one knows who the Father is except the Son and those to whom the Son chooses to reveal him."

Then he turned to his disciples and said privately, "Blessed are the eyes that see what you see. For I tell you that many prophets and kings wanted to see what you see but did not see it, and to hear what you hear but did not hear it."

Consider This

Okay, let's kick off the day with a good old-fashioned pop quiz. Only one question: How many distinct prayers do we have recorded coming from the mouth of Jesus?

Now, to be fair I'm going to make this an open book quiz and give you until tomorrow to come up with the answer. And I'll give you a head start. Today's text gives us one of those prayers.

I praise you, Father, Lord of heaven and earth, because you have hidden these things from the wise and learned, and revealed them to little children. Yes, Father, for this is what you were pleased to do.

Let's get the bigger picture of what's going on in the text today. Jesus is enjoying a Holy Spirit joy explosion. Think of it as a divine end-zone dance after a game-winning touchdown. Had high-fives and chest-bumps been invented back then, Jesus and the Seventy-Two would have been doing them at this point in the story. The Seventy-Two were telling stories of crushing demons (note the explicit qualifier, "in your name"). Jesus speaks of his seeing "Satan fall like lightning from heaven." Somewhere over on the sidelines, Team Satan were working the referees for an excessive celebration penalty—to no avail.

This exuberant celebration marks the successful transferability of the authority of Jesus to other people. I mean, it wasn't a sure thing, was it? Something tells me Jesus may have been holding his breath a little bit. Would these men and women actually be able to operate in the gifted authority of the Son of God? Their coming back with this news was a big deal. In the midst of it all, Jesus couldn't even contain the joy. He wanted the Father to share in this signal moment of celebration. In what clearly ranks as his most exuberantly joyful prayer, he shouted out, *I praise you, Father, Lord of heaven and earth, because you have hidden these things from the wise and learned, and revealed them to little children. Yes, Father, for this is what you were pleased to do.*

I call this one "The Prayer of Great Reversal." Jesus is turning the world upside down—no, right side up. The kingdom is breaking in, and the underdogs are winning. Let's take a closer look at the prayer.

It looks like the "wise and learned" are taking it on the chin. Wouldn't that be a good thing—to be wise and learned? Rather than good or bad, I think the issue is one of danger. The great danger of becoming wise and learned is of turning wisdom and learning into a form of status and prestige. You know the familiar saying, "Knowledge is power." It's true. Will my or your learnedness or expertise be for us a source of pride or humility? And that all depends on how we understand from whence our learning and wisdom comes. Watch where Jesus takes it next: *All things have been committed to me by my Father. No one knows who the Son is except the Father, and no one knows who the Father is except the Son and those to whom the Son chooses to reveal him.*

Divine revelation is not a product of religious study. Divine revelation is the fruit of a devoted relationship. Don't hear me wrong. Study is a given. It's just a question of whether study finds its roots in a relationship characterized by loving devotion or proceeds from a self-determined pursuit to gain power, prestige, or position. We all know people, pastors, scholars, and leaders on both sides of that equation.

It's why the Bible says over and over and over things like, "God opposes the proud but gives grace to the humble" (James 4:6 ESV).

Dr. Luke, our guide through the gospel, is a great example of one whose wisdom and learning have come in the relationship way of a disciple of Jesus.

So back to the open book quiz we opened with today about the prayers of Jesus. Rather than jumping to Google or concordances or Bible dictionaries or power-scanning the pages of your Bible, try this. Ask God to fill you with the Holy Spirit in such a way as to reveal and remind you of Jesus' various prayers. Be still before him and rehearse the story of the gospel in your mind's eye. See what comes. This is the stuff of a devoted relationship. From this holy groundedness, it's no holds barred. Go for it.

And don't forget to read Jesus' most exuberant prayer out loud today. Invite the Holy Spirit to fill you with joyful exuberance in doing so.

The Prayer

Lord Jesus Christ, Son of God, have mercy on me, a sinner.
Lord Jesus Christ, Son of God, have mercy on me, a son/daughter.
Lord Jesus Christ, Son of God, have mercy on me, a saint.

The Question

How important is it to you to be known as a knowledge-able or learned person? Why does that matter so much in the world's value system? Why might our humility be more important to Jesus?

Do Good

5

LUKE 10:25–37 | On one occasion an expert in the law stood up to test Jesus. "Teacher," he asked, "what must I do to inherit eternal life?"

"What is written in the Law?" he replied. "How do you read it?"

He answered, "'Love the Lord your God with all your heart and with all your soul and with all your strength and with all your mind'; and, 'Love your neighbor as yourself.'"

"You have answered correctly," Jesus replied. "Do this and you will live."

But he wanted to justify himself, so he asked Jesus, "And who is my neighbor?"

In reply Jesus said: "A man was going down from Jerusalem to Jericho, when he was attacked by robbers. They stripped him of his clothes, beat him and went away, leaving him half dead. A priest happened to be going down the same road, and when he saw the man, he passed by on the other side. So too, a Levite, when he came to the place and saw him, passed by on the other side. But a Samaritan, as he traveled, came where the man was; and when he saw him, he took pity on him. He went to him and bandaged his wounds, pouring on oil and wine. Then he put the man on his own donkey, brought him to an inn and took care of him. The next day he took out two denarii and gave them to the innkeeper. 'Look after him,' he said, 'and when I return, I will reimburse you for any extra expense you may have.'

"Which of these three do you think was a neighbor to the man who fell into the hands of robbers?"

The expert in the law replied, "The one who had mercy on him."

Jesus told him, "Go and do likewise."

Consider This

Before we begin with today's text, I want to share the answer to yesterday's pop quiz. How many distinct prayers do we have recorded from the mouth of Jesus? Answer: nine. See appendix A for the prayers.

Now to today's text, which demonstrates the sheer brilliance of Jesus.

The expert in the law comes to test one he calls the teacher. He sees in Jesus a peer of sorts. He is about to get schooled.

On one occasion an expert in the law stood up to test Jesus. "Teacher," he asked, "what must I do to inherit eternal life?"

Note how Jesus immediately turns the test around by asking the expert in the law about his own subject matter. Jesus refuses to play defense. It's a good lesson for his followers.

"What is written in the Law?" he replied. "How do you read it?"

He takes the bait—hook, line, and sinker. Eager to get it right, he responds, *"'Love the Lord your God with all your heart and with all your soul and with all your strength and with all your mind'; and, 'Love your neighbor as yourself.'"*

Jesus gives him an A with a short teacher's note to the effect of, "It's not enough to get the answer right. You have to actually do it." He seems prepared to leave it at that.

"You have answered correctly," Jesus replied. "Do this and you will live."

As far as Jesus is concerned, it's class dismissed. The expert, however, can't leave it alone. Remember, he's trying to test the "Teacher."

But he wanted to justify himself, so he asked Jesus, "And who is my neighbor?"

Here's what I think he was asking: Who is not my neighbor? These first-century lawyer types wanted to determine who they didn't have to love. Just like with the Sabbath, and their focus on the meaning of the word *work*, this time it was the word *neighbor*. They wanted to prove their perfect compliance with the demands of the Law (i.e., to justify themselves).

In my peripheral vision I can see the disciples off to the side turning to one another with wincing looks of, "He just said the wrong thing!" "The expert is about to get it handed to him."

Rather than a frontal smackdown assault, Jesus lays a story trap. He will lead this expert down a path where he will be confronted with the absurdity of his own outlook.

"A man was going down from Jerusalem to Jericho, when he was attacked by robbers. They stripped him of his clothes, beat him and went away, leaving him half dead."

A man is all we get. Attacked, robbed, stripped, beaten, and left for dead.

"A priest happened to be going down the same road, and when he saw the man, he passed by on the other side. So too, a Levite, when he came to the place and saw him, passed by on the other side."

The expert's notion of the Law is under scrutiny now. Of course, the priest and the Levite couldn't get near this guy. It would make them ceremonially unclean, which would prevent them from performing their religious responsibilities in the temple (heaven forbid!). The Law, meant to illuminate all of life, had through their misguided interpretation become the source of their blindness. The priest and the Levite saw the bleeding man. The trouble was they didn't have eyes to see him.

At the same time, the expert is confronted with the urgency of the life-and-death situation at hand. Somebody needs to help this poor soul. He's probably asking himself W.W.M.D.? (What would Moses do?). Jesus, the Master Storyteller, artfully dances with the expert like a prize fighter. Jab. Jab. Jab.

"But a Samaritan, as he traveled, came where the man was; and when he saw him, he took pity on him."

BOOM! Right hook! But a Samaritan . . . Really?! The expert's jaw drops, but Jesus doesn't indict him just yet with the neighbor question. What fascinates me is what Jesus doesn't do here. If I were telling the story, I might just leave it at, "he took pity on him," and moved on quickly to the gotcha part. Instead, Jesus goes for the love part. He proceeds to reveal the extravagance of divine love in ordinary human form. I want you to see this. I'm going to enumerate and list for effect.

(1) He went to him and bandaged his wounds, (2) pouring on oil and wine. (3) Then he put the man on his own donkey, (4) brought him to an inn, and (5) took care of him. (6) The next day he took out two denarii and gave them to the innkeeper. (7) "Look after him," he said, "and (8) when I return, I will reimburse you for any extra expense you may have."

All this time I'm thinking the neighbor is the guy who got beat up and left for dead. Jesus completely flips it.

"Which of these three do you think was a neighbor to the man who fell into the hands of robbers?"

This is not a question of who is my neighbor. The big question is, How can I be a neighbor? In a stroke of divine irony, this story shows us that the natural heirs of the kingdom of God least resemble the righteousness of God, and the avowed enemies of the heirs of the kingdom are lifted up as the exemplars of God's righteousness.

The expert in the law replied, "The one who had mercy on him."

Jesus, 1. Expert, 0.

And just when Jesus could really excoriate the guy (like he did a couple of days ago with his rant against Chorazin and Bethsaida and Capernaum), he has mercy on him with a word of grace. Listen to him . . .

Jesus told him, "Go and do likewise."

It's not a question of who is or is not my neighbor. The question is, What kind of neighbor will I be?

Do good, and always remember that goodness is as goodness does.

The Prayer

Lord Jesus Christ, Son of God, have mercy on me, a sinner.
Lord Jesus Christ, Son of God, have mercy on me, a son/daughter.
Lord Jesus Christ, Son of God, have mercy on me, a saint.

The Question

On a scale of 1–10 (10 is highest), where do you rate yourself on needing to justify yourself before others? Are you a person who needs to be right most of the time—in a conflict or argument?

Beware of Self-Serving Service

6

LUKE 10:38–42 | As Jesus and his disciples were on their way, he came to a village where a woman named Martha opened her home to him. She had a sister called Mary, who sat at the Lord's feet listening to what he said. But Martha was distracted by all the preparations that had to be made. She came to him and asked, "Lord, don't you care that my sister has left me to do the work by myself? Tell her to help me!"

"Martha, Martha," the Lord answered, "you are worried and upset about many things, but few things are needed—or indeed only one. Mary has chosen what is better, and it will not be taken away from her."

Consider This

A woman's place is in . . .

For centuries this text has been used to create a dichotomy between prayer and action; to show how the contemplative life is better than the activist life; to extol the life of prayer over the life of busyness. To shame Martha and champion Mary.

I'm going to cut to the chase here and try to make the case for a better interpretation of the passage.

The big issue is hospitality. On the face of it, one would expect Martha to win the prize. I mean she is hustling around like a crazy woman who just found out a dozen men and the Son of God invited themselves over for dinner.

On the surface, Martha appears like the hostess with the most-est. Note, though, the key word from today's text: *But Martha was distracted by all the preparations that had to be made.*

There it is. The difference between Mary and Martha isn't really about contemplation versus activism. It's about attention and distraction.

I contend that Martha's problem isn't what she's doing but how she's doing it. Sometimes hospitality is about the guest, and other times it's about the host. Notice the personal pronouns in Martha's words to Jesus.

She came to him and asked, "Lord, don't you care that my sister has left me to do the work by myself? Tell her to help me!"

There it is. Me, myself, and my and one more me. This time, it looks like the hospitality was more about Martha, the hostess, than Jesus, the guest. Martha was seized by worry and anxiety, which always turns whatever focus we had on others right back onto ourselves. Listen to him: *"Martha, Martha," the Lord answered, "you are worried and upset about many things, but few things are needed—or indeed only one. Mary has chosen what is better, and it will not be taken away from her."*

So what one needful thing did Mary choose? It's right there in the text a sentence or two back. *She had a sister called Mary, who sat at the Lord's feet listening to what he said.*

Do you see it? Mary chose the one necessary thing: *listening to him.* Remember Transfiguration Mountain and that Word from God? This is that.

Mary, 1. Martha, 0.

It's more than an aside, but I want to reference the radical move Jesus makes here. Jesus basically tells us that a woman's place is not in the kitchen but in his presence. Mary was a woman, doing what men would customarily do in the first century (i.e., sitting at Jesus' feet); that's the thing that wouldn't be taken away from her as much as Martha might have wished it. And that's an aside within this aside— sometimes the greatest enemies of women taking their rightful place of discipleship and authority in the church (and in the world) are other women.

Perhaps this is conjecture, but I think Jesus is not dissing Martha's hospitality as much as he is critiquing it. There is a way of serving one's self under the cloak of serving others. It's all about appearances, perfection, and performance. Perhaps Martha's sense of self and worth were all wrapped up in properly performing her role while Mary's sense of herself was all wrapped up in her relationship to Jesus.

The Prayer

Lord Jesus Christ, Son of God, have mercy on me, a sinner.
Lord Jesus Christ, Son of God, have mercy on me, a
*   son/daughter.*
Lord Jesus Christ, Son of God, have mercy on me, a saint.

The Question

Have you discovered yet how your service toward others can be more about you than them? Why is that?

7 Learn the Prayer—It's Better than Yours

LUKE 11:1–4 | One day Jesus was praying in a certain place. When he finished, one of his disciples said to him, "Lord, teach us to pray, just as John taught his disciples."

He said to them, "When you pray, say:

"'Father,
hallowed be your name,
your kingdom come.
Give us each day our daily bread.
Forgive us our sins,
for we also forgive everyone who sins against us.
And lead us not into temptation.'"

Consider This

As I have tried to listen to Jesus through these days of Lent, I am learning things I have never understood before. The interesting thing about understanding is there's always more to be had. The life, words, deeds, miracles, signs, moves, death, resurrection, and ascension of Jesus is ever revealing more truth and releasing more meaning. Remember, he reveals in the midst of relationship.

Today's text brings us to the famed Lord's Prayer. Let's work to listen to him as he teaches us to pray.

I used to think the measure of a prayer was the sincerity of the one praying. While sincerity is surely a good thing, I now think the measure of a prayer is its substance. This prayer Jesus teaches us is so stocked and layered with substance, I am convinced we will never exhaust it all.

I want to share some insights that are coming to me as I try to listen and learn from Jesus in this prayer.

He said to them, "When you pray, say: "'Father . . .

Prayer begins with knowing what to call God. There are so many names by which God is called in Scripture. He is Yahweh, Elohim, Jehovah, Adonai, and on we could go. My late grandmother-in-law once gave me a book entitled *The 365 Wonderful Names of Our Wonderful Lord*. The interesting thing we learn from Jesus is how Jesus doesn't call God by name but according to their relationship: Father. He invites us into his extraordinary relationship with his Father which graces us to say, "Our Father." In life, we call just about everyone by their name, except when it comes to our parents. As my children are growing up, life is constantly changing. Our relationship seems to change by the day as they mature. What most pleases me is what hasn't changed. They still call me "Da-Da." That's not a name. It's a term of profound endearment. Jesus actually used the term *Abba*, an exquisitely intimate and endearing term.

So he teaches us to address God in terms of our relation to him and not by a name, and then, interestingly enough, he says this: *"Hallowed be your name."* We are about to find out just who our Father happens to be. The God we are privileged to call Father, actually has the most holy name ever uttered. In fact (if I am remembering right), the people of Israel so lived in awe of the name of God they would not speak it except by the high priest once a year on the Day of Atonement. By teaching us to hallow the name of God, Jesus reminds us that though we call God by this intimate term of relationship, we must remember that our Father is the King of the universe, the Creator of all that is, and the righteous Judge, who lives in heaven. This God, who is our intimate Father, happens to be the high and exalted Creator of the heavens and the earth.

Watch what happens now. What I have always understood to be a series of essential petitions, I am now beginning to see as so much more. Rather than a series of asks, this prayer is a full-court celebration of our entire relationship with God. Because God is our Father, everything else that God is becomes a gift to us.

When we say, "Your kingdom come," we are declaring our Father as the King of the universe.

When we say, "Give us each day our daily bread," we are declaring our Father as Jehovah-Jireh, our Provider.

When we say, "Forgive us our sins [or trespasses]," we are declaring our Father as merciful Judge and a gracious healer.

When we say, "Lead us not into temptation," we are declaring our Father as Mighty Deliverer and Protector.

I am beginning to understand the Lord's Prayer not so much as a collection of petitions but as a profoundly powerful declaration of faith.

And it all comes together in the word *Father*. In fact, when we speak this term to God in prayer, we are saying all of this and more. Not only does Jesus teach us to call God "Father," he shows us exactly what a true and loving Father looks like. For the many whose fathers served as a source of brokenness, Jesus reveals a Father who will heal with blessedness. Jesus brings all the attributes, character, roles, and names of God under the covering of a perfect Father.

Rather than a rote recitation, the Lord's Prayer is a revelatory declaration. If I will really listen to him, this is how I will now pray. I will rely more on the substance of Jesus teaching and training than on my best efforts at sincerity. In fact, I think this is the substance that creates true sincerity.

Closing thought: Jesus is teaching us to pray with divine substance. When we put substance ahead of sincerity, our faith will begin to form our feelings. When we put sincerity ahead of substance, we will depend on our feelings to form our faith.

The Prayer

Lord Jesus Christ, Son of God, have mercy on me, a sinner.
Lord Jesus Christ, Son of God, have mercy on me, a son/daughter.
Lord Jesus Christ, Son of God, have mercy on me, a saint.

The Question

Where are you in your relationship with God as Father? Is it real or religious-ish? What would help you grow here?

8 | Ask Our Father for the Gift of the Holy Spirit

LUKE 11:5–13 | Then Jesus said to them, "Suppose you have a friend, and you go to him at midnight and say, 'Friend, lend me three loaves of bread; a friend of mine on a journey has come to me, and I have no food to offer him.' And suppose the one inside answers, 'Don't bother me. The door is already locked, and my children and I are in bed. I can't get up and give you anything.' I tell you, even though he will not get up and give you the bread because of friendship, yet because of your shameless audacity he will surely get up and give you as much as you need.

"So I say to you: Ask and it will be given to you; seek and you will find; knock and the door will be opened to you. For everyone who asks receives; the one who seeks finds; and to the one who knocks, the door will be opened.

"Which of you fathers, if your son asks for a fish, will give him a snake instead? Or if he asks for an egg, will give him a scorpion? If you then, though you are evil, know how to give good gifts to your children, how much more will your Father in heaven give the Holy Spirit to those who ask him!"

Consider This

Three words capture today's text. Did you hear them? I'm not referring to, "Ask, seek, and knock." For me, the three words are, "How much more?"

Jesus seems to have one major agenda in his teaching about prayer. It's not about technique. Jesus' singular agenda is to reveal what God is like. You remember a few days back when Jesus said this, "No one knows who the Son is except the Father, or who the Father is except the Son and anyone to whom the Son chooses to reveal him" (Luke 10:22 ESV).

This is what he's up to here.

Example #1: A friend comes to your house in the middle of the night needing help. You can't help but you know I can, so you come to my house. I don't want to go to the trouble to get out of bed—even though I am supposedly your friend. The only reason I ultimately get up and help is because you are so stinking, shamelessly loud that you are going to wake up the entire neighborhood.

The point? God is nothing like this. If this friend who doesn't really care gets out of bed to help—how much more will our Father come to our aid? No need for shameless audacity. Just ask, seek, and knock.

Example #2: No father, even the worst, would give their child poison when they asked for milk. So even if the worst will do good for their children, how much more will our Father in heaven?

Jesus wants us to share his confidence in his Father and ours. He's basically saying, "God, our Father, is so much better than the best you can possibly imagine, I can't possibly fully get it across to you because you don't even have the categories to process it. How much more?"

"How much more will your Father in heaven give the Holy Spirit to those who ask him?"

Our Father gives us daily bread, forgiveness, peace, protection, deliverance, and more, but how much more will he give us the Holy Spirit, the gift of himself, his presence, nearer than our breath. Again, our Father is better than the best we can possibly imagine and even better than that.

So I ask you, Have you asked him to give you the Holy Spirit? Today?

> For you did not receive the spirit of slavery to fall back into fear, but you have received the Spirit of adoption as sons, by whom we cry, "Abba! Father!" The Spirit himself bears witness with our spirit that we are children of God. (Rom. 8:15–16 ESV)

If we listen to Jesus, we will ask our Father to give us the Holy Spirit. That's the call to action today. Same thing tomorrow. And the day after that.

The Prayer

Lord Jesus Christ, Son of God, have mercy on me, a sinner.
Lord Jesus Christ, Son of God, have mercy on me, a son/daughter.
Lord Jesus Christ, Son of God, have mercy on me, a saint.

The Question

When is the last time you asked our Father to give you the Holy Spirit? How frequently do you ask him? Why or why not?

Give up the Quest for Middle Ground

9

LUKE 11:14–28 ESV | Now he was casting out a demon that was mute. When the demon had gone out, the mute man spoke, and the people marveled. But some of them said, "He casts out demons by Beelzebul, the prince of demons," while others, to test him, kept seeking from him a sign from heaven. But he, knowing their thoughts, said to them, "Every kingdom divided against itself is laid waste, and a divided household falls. And if Satan also is divided against himself, how will his kingdom stand? For you say that I cast out demons by Beelzebul. And if I cast out demons by Beelzebul, by whom do your sons cast them out? Therefore they will be your judges. But if it is by the finger of God that I cast out demons, then the kingdom of God has come upon you. When a strong man, fully armed, guards his own palace, his goods are safe; but when one stronger than he attacks him and overcomes him, he takes away his armor in which he trusted and divides his spoil. Whoever is not with me is against me, and whoever does not gather with me scatters.

"When the unclean spirit has gone out of a person, it passes through waterless places seeking rest, and finding none it says, 'I will return to my house from which I came.' And when it comes, it finds the house swept and put in order. Then it goes and brings seven other spirits more evil than itself, and they enter and dwell there. And the last state of that person is worse than the first."

As he said these things, a woman in the crowd raised her voice and said to him, "Blessed is the womb that bore you, and the breasts at which you nursed!" But he said, "Blessed rather are those who hear the word of God and keep it!"

Consider This

I'm going to cut to the chase today.

There is only one secure place to stand in this crazy world and that is "with me," Jesus says. But if you are not actually with me, then you are against me. If you are not building what I am building, then you are tearing it down.

There is no middle ground. This is really hard teaching. It is so seductive to think we can live in this mushy, moderate, middle place. We can't, because it's not a real place. There is either "with me," or "against me."

Jesus makes it pretty clear what he means by us being "with him."

But he said, "Blessed rather are those who hear the word of God and [obey] it."

We either hear the Word of God and obey it or we don't. There is no middle ground. If there's one thing we can say of the Word of God, it is consistent.

> "Everyone then who hears these words of mine and does them will be like a wise man who built his house on the rock. And the rain fell, and the floods came, and the winds blew and beat on that house, but it did not fall, because it had its foundation on the rock. And everyone who hears these words of mine and does not

do them will be like a foolish man who built his house on the sand. And the rain fell, and the floods came, and the winds blew and beat against that house, and it fell, and great was the fall of it." (Matt. 7:24–27 ESV)

What good is it, my brothers, if someone says he has faith but does not have works? Can that faith save him? If a brother or a sister is poorly clothed and lacking in daily food, and one of you says to them, "Go in peace, be warmed and filled," without giving them the things needed for the body, what good is that? So also faith by itself, if it does not have works, is dead. (James 2:14–17 ESV)

"I know your works: you are neither cold nor hot. Would that you were either cold or hot! So, because you are lukewarm, and neither hot nor cold, I will spit you out of my mouth." (Rev. 3:15–16 ESV)

But be doers of the word, and not hearers only, deceiving yourselves. (James 1:22 ESV)

So we have a choice, and the prior texts make clear the choice has consequences. I think that's what this conversation in today's text is getting at. The big problem of not being "with him," which is to say not obeying the Word of God, is it leaves us open to all sorts of danger. Jesus can deliver a person from an impure spirit, but he will not make a person obey the Word of God. If a person delivered from an impure spirit does not obey the Word of God, they leave themselves open to an even worse infestation of evil and darkness. It's either repent or relapse. A clean swept house must now be furnished with obedience to the Word of God.

In all of these texts, we aren't given threats but bottom line realities.

With each step toward the cross, Jesus takes us deeper into the discipleship of his commitment to us. He teaches us that the sign that we are truly listening to him is obeying what we hear. There is a word for this so-called middle ground of listening to him and not obeying. The word is *disobedience*.

It makes sense. Don't you think?

These days of Lent are intended for the kind of inner examination (not to be confused with morbid introspection) wherein we open ourselves to a deeper repentance—a closer alignment of our lives with his Word. Introspection is something we do to ourselves. It's not to be confused with inner examination, which is something the Holy Spirit does. It happens when we pray like this and mean it:

> Search me, O God, and know my heart!
>> Try me and know my thoughts!
> And see if there be any grievous way in me,
>> and lead me in the way everlasting. (Ps. 139:23–24 ESV)

The Prayer
Lord Jesus Christ, Son of God, have mercy on me, a sinner.
Lord Jesus Christ, Son of God, have mercy on me, a son/daughter.
Lord Jesus Christ, Son of God, have mercy on me, a saint.

The Question

Have you considered the reality of Jesus' commitment to you as a disciple? We mostly think of it as our commitment. Where do you struggle with obedience?

Flip Repentance

LUKE 11:29–32 ESV | When the crowds were increasing, he began to say, "This generation is an evil generation. It seeks for a sign, but no sign will be given to it except the sign of Jonah. For as Jonah became a sign to the people of Nineveh, so will the Son of Man be to this generation. The queen of the South will rise up at the judgment with the men of this generation and condemn them, for she came from the ends of the earth to hear the wisdom of Solomon, and behold, something greater than Solomon is here. The men of Nineveh will rise up at the judgment with this generation and condemn it, for they repented at the preaching of Jonah, and behold, something greater than Jonah is here.

Consider This

Jesus attracted lots of window shoppers but few buyers. It explains why he would say such a thing to a growing crowd, calling them a wicked generation. Crowds want to be impressed. They want a sign. Why is that so wicked? Think back. That's actually what Satan asked Jesus for in the desert. He wanted a sign that Jesus was who he said he was.

Jesus, steeped in Scripture as he was, dials up Jonah. What is the meaning of the sign of Jonah? Jonah preached to the wicked generation in Ninevah, and they repented. They not only heard the word of God, but they obeyed it.

Jesus is growing weary of the crowds. They want signs, more revelation. Jesus is looking for repentance.

Jonah offers another sign. He was in the belly of the great fish for three days, and soon we will witness the great sign of the third day: the resurrection.

As we get nearer to Jerusalem, things are going to heat up. We will be surprised at who hears Jesus' words and steps out of the crowd to heed his invitation. They will show us what repentance looks like. So often we think repentance needs to be some dramatic sin we need to cease doing or some kind of bad behavior we need to turn away from. To be sure, that may be the case. For many, if not most, of you who are reading the Daily Text, this is probably not the case. Far more likely is this slipping into and out of the crowd. Faith is neither hot nor cold, but somewhere in between. Rather than some clear-cut form of behavior modification, what may be called for is a bold run toward Jesus. The gravity of the crowd is strong. It will take an escape velocity fueled by the Holy Spirit to break free. What might it look like to risk in these days of Lent? What might it look like to quietly leave the crowd and find a closer walk with Jesus?

As we near Jerusalem, we must think of repentance in terms of who we are running to more than what we turn away from. It's time to flip repentance.

The Prayer

Lord Jesus Christ, Son of God, have mercy on me, a sinner.
Lord Jesus Christ, Son of God, have mercy on me, a
son/daughter.
Lord Jesus Christ, Son of God, have mercy on me, a saint.

The Question

How is repentance in your life taking the shape of what you are running toward? How strong is the gravity of the luke-warm crowd in your present life and faith?

Second Sunday of Lent

Pursue Gut-Level Honesty

LUKE 11:33–36 | "No one lights a lamp and puts it in a place where it will be hidden, or under a bowl. Instead they put it on its stand, so that those who come in may see the light. Your eye is the lamp of your body. When your eyes are healthy, your whole body also is full of light. But when they are unhealthy, your body also is full of darkness. See to it, then, that the light within you is not darkness. Therefore, if your whole body is full of light, and no part of it dark, it will be just as full of light as when a lamp shines its light on you."

Consider This

The first century understood eyesight differently than we do today. The health of one's eyes reflected the interior condition of a person. If their eyes were unhealthy, it was symptomatic of their interior life being dark. The eye, Jesus says, is the lamp of the body. The light or lack thereof comes from within a person and shines through their eyes.

"When your eyes are healthy, your whole body also is full of light."

The gospel means change from the inside out. Broken human nature wants to try to cover over the darkness within by creating a shiny surface. As we get closer and closer to the cross, Jesus will confront us with just this reality. He is looking for a radiance that comes from the deepest place in a person. In fact, he is looking for a quality of inner light and life that only he is capable of putting there.

This is why he calls us to follow him. On another occasion, he made this abundantly clear, "I am the light of the world. Whoever follows me will not walk in darkness, but will have the light of life" (John 8:12 ESV).

Referencing this very thing, the apostle Paul wrote these words: "For God, who said, 'Let light shine out of darkness,' has shone in our hearts to give us the light of the knowledge of the glory of God in the face of Christ" (2 Cor. 4:6 ESV).

Jesus can work with human darkness. What he can't tolerate are people who try to counterfeit the light by their false appearances. Jesus delights in humble honesty. He detests hypocrisy.

Human beings have an almost infinite capacity for self-deception. It's why we are giving ourselves to praying the Jesus Prayer, this ancient prayer that will itself lead us to the cross. I want to urge you to take it not only to heart but to the streets—through your steps. It's not one of the nine prayers of Jesus, but it may very well be the single most important prayer to him.

I'll see you tomorrow at dinner with a group who refused to learn this prayer. It will not be pretty.

The Prayer

Lord Jesus Christ, Son of God, have mercy on me, a sinner.

*Lord Jesus Christ, Son of God, have mercy on me, a
son/daughter.
Lord Jesus Christ, Son of God, have mercy on me, a saint.*

The Question

How deep is your desire for this inner radiance of the goodness of God (a.k.a. holiness) in your life? What seems more
appealing to you than this?

Take the Inside-Out Route

LUKE 11:37–52 | When Jesus had finished speaking, a
Pharisee invited him to eat with him; so he went in and
reclined at the table. But the Pharisee was surprised when he
noticed that Jesus did not first wash before the meal.

Then the Lord said to him, "Now then, you Pharisees clean the
outside of the cup and dish, but inside you are full of greed and
wickedness. You foolish people! Did not the one who made the
outside make the inside also? But now as for what is inside
you—be generous to the poor, and everything will be clean
for you.

"Woe to you Pharisees, because you give God a tenth of your
mint, rue and all other kinds of garden herbs, but you neglect
justice and the love of God. You should have practiced the latter
without leaving the former undone.

"Woe to you Pharisees, because you love the most important seats in the synagogues and respectful greetings in the marketplaces.

"Woe to you, because you are like unmarked graves, which people walk over without knowing it."

One of the experts in the law answered him, "Teacher, when you say these things, you insult us also."

Jesus replied, "And you experts in the law, woe to you, because you load people down with burdens they can hardly carry, and you yourselves will not lift one finger to help them.

"Woe to you, because you build tombs for the prophets, and it was your ancestors who killed them. So you testify that you approve of what your ancestors did; they killed the prophets, and you build their tombs. Because of this, God in his wisdom said, 'I will send them prophets and apostles, some of whom they will kill and others they will persecute.' Therefore this generation will be held responsible for the blood of all the prophets that has been shed since the beginning of the world, from the blood of Abel to the blood of Zechariah, who was killed between the altar and the sanctuary. Yes, I tell you, this generation will be held responsible for it all."

Woe to you experts in the law, because you have taken away the key to knowledge. You yourselves have not entered, and you have hindered those who were entering."

Consider This

Lord Jesus Christ, Son of God, have mercy on me, a sinner. Are you staying with it? I'm not going to leave you alone about it. I want this to become the prayer of your heart. I want you to understand, though, that this is not a self-deprecating prayer. To say you are a sinner is not to shame yourself as a bad person. It is to come to grips with the fact that you (and I) are a broken person. We aren't necessarily broken by anything we have done—though those things we have done and left undone have certainly contributed to our brokenness. You and I are broken by virtue of being a member of the human race. We are not sinners because we sin. We sin because we are sinners.

There are two basic ways to approach righteousness. There's the outside-in approach and the inside-out approach. External conformity to the law by performance versus internal fulfillment of the law by grace. This outside-in approach captures the methodology of the Pharisees. The inside-out approach captures the way of Jesus. The Pharisees concerned themselves with clean hands. Jesus was after a pure heart. It seems to me the Pharisees were all about rightness, while Jesus was all about goodness.

Then the Lord said to him, "Now then, you Pharisees clean the outside of the cup and dish, but inside you are full of greed and wickedness. You foolish people! Did not the one who made the outside make the inside also? But now as for what is inside you— be generous to the poor, and everything will be clean for you."

The Pharisees show us that sometimes you can get it all right and be all wrong.

"*Woe to you Pharisees, because you give God a tenth of your mint, rue and all other kinds of garden herbs, but you neglect justice and the love of God. You should have practiced the latter without leaving the former undone.*"

The outside-in approach of the Pharisees tries to cover over brokenness. The inside-out approach of Jesus aims to transform it.

And that raises the biggest problem. As long as we are trying to cover our brokenness we cannot be healed. But the minute we become honest about the fundamental problem of our brokenness (i.e., I am a sinner), grace will not only save us but make us into the people we most want to become.

Bringing it full circle—this is why the Jesus Prayer matters so much. "Lord Jesus Christ, Son of God, have mercy on me, a sinner."

Stay with it.

The Prayer

Lord Jesus Christ, Son of God, have mercy on me, a sinner.
Lord Jesus Christ, Son of God, have mercy on me, a son/daughter.
Lord Jesus Christ, Son of God, have mercy on me, a saint.

The Question

Are you coming to grips with your brokenness as a member of the human race, or are you still trying to cover it over yourself? What about that?

Realize Your Influence

12

LUKE 11:53–12:12 | When Jesus went outside, the Pharisees and the teachers of the law began to oppose him fiercely and to besiege him with questions, waiting to catch him in something he might say.

Meanwhile, when a crowd of many thousands had gathered, so that they were trampling on one another, Jesus began to speak first to his disciples, saying: "Be on your guard against the yeast of the Pharisees, which is hypocrisy. There is nothing concealed that will not be disclosed, or hidden that will not be made known. What you have said in the dark will be heard in the daylight, and what you have whispered in the ear in the inner rooms will be proclaimed from the roofs.

"I tell you, my friends, do not be afraid of those who kill the body and after that can do no more. But I will show you whom you should fear: Fear him who, after your body has been killed, has authority to throw you into hell. Yes, I tell you, fear him. Are not five sparrows sold for two pennies? Yet not one of them is forgotten by God. Indeed, the very hairs of your head are all numbered. Don't be afraid; you are worth more than many sparrows.

"I tell you, whoever publicly acknowledges me before others, the Son of Man will also acknowledge before the angels of God. But whoever disowns me before others will be disowned before the angels of God. And everyone who speaks a word against the Son of Man will be forgiven, but anyone who blasphemes against the Holy Spirit will not be forgiven.

"When you are brought before synagogues, rulers and authorities, do not worry about how you will defend yourselves or what you will say, for the Holy Spirit will teach you at that time what you should say."

Consider This

Yeast is a good thing . . . until it's not. Jesus utilized the metaphor of yeast on more than one occasion to teach his disciples. You remember the time he said, "The kingdom of heaven is like yeast that a woman took and mixed into about sixty pounds of flour until it worked all through the dough" (Matt. 13:33).

Yeast is like an almost invisible dust. A little yeast goes a long way. It has an inordinate influence on anything it touches. Yeast works like a change agent. Put yeast into dough and it causes the dough to rise. Put yeast into crushed grape juice and it causes fermentation, becoming wine. In this little parable, Jesus says the kingdom of heaven is like yeast. It is almost invisible to the human eye and yet when it gets mixed into the world, it creates a highly visible effect. In this case, a small bit of yeast is worked into a massive amount of dough, which will lead to an abundance of bread. How does something so small go so far and do so much? That's the point.

Yeast is a type of change agent. The question: Is this good change or bad change? Bottom line: people are like yeast. As change agents, will we be charged with the kingdom of God or with hypocrisy? For better or for worse, a few people can have a massive impact on an entire community. We all know this is true in our experience of others, but we rarely believe it could be true of ourselves.

Hypocrisy is maintaining an outward appearance that masks over the inward reality. So if hypocrisy is the mark of the Pharisees, what is the defining characteristic of the kingdom of God? How about authenticity?

Keeping it real (and short), let's ask ourselves the question: Which kind of yeast am I? What kind of change am I effecting in the people around me?

And let's be reminded—Jesus issued this stern warning: *"Be on your guard against the yeast of the Pharisees, which is hypocrisy."*

The Prayer

Lord Jesus Christ, Son of God, have mercy on me, a sinner.
Lord Jesus Christ, Son of God, have mercy on me, a
  son/daughter.
Lord Jesus Christ, Son of God, have mercy on me, a saint.

The Question

Which kind of yeast am I? What kind of change am I effecting in the people around me?

13 Be Possessed by Abundance

LUKE 12:13–21 ESV | Someone in the crowd said to him, "Teacher, tell my brother to divide the inheritance with me." But he said to him, "Man, who made me a judge or arbitrator over you?" And he said to them, "Take care, and be on your guard against all covetousness, for one's life does not consist in the abundance of his possessions." And he told them a parable, saying, "The land of a rich man produced plentifully, and he thought to himself, 'What shall I do, for I have nowhere to store my crops?' And he said, 'I will do this: I will tear down my barns and build larger ones, and there I will store all my grain and my goods. And I will say to my soul, "Soul, you have ample goods laid up for many years; relax, eat, drink, be merry."' But God said to him, 'Fool! This night your soul is required of you, and the things you have prepared, whose will they be?' So is the one who lays up treasure for himself and is not rich toward God."

Consider This

When we pray, "Lord Jesus Christ, Son of God, have mercy on me, a sinner," we must ask, What is mercy? Jesus died on the cross for our sins so we could have eternal life. Yes, that's mercy, but mercy is far more expansive. I like the way Paul put it in his letter to the Romans: "For if while we were enemies we were reconciled to God by the death of his Son, much more, now that we are reconciled, shall we be saved by his life!" (5:10 ESV).

The entire life of the eternal Son of God is the mercy of God. His conception, birth, life, words, teaching, healing, signs, miracles, suffering, death, burial, resurrection, ascension, and return: all the mercy of God.

This warning yesterday to "Be on your guard against the yeast of the Pharisees, which is hypocrisy," is a merciful word from God. Jesus knows where all the land mines are buried along the pathway of human life. He knows all the temp-tations, pitfalls, and problems, and he mercifully teaches us how to steer clear of such disasters. This prayer, "Lord Jesus Christ, Son of God, have mercy on me, a sinner," prepares us to recognize mercy when it appears and to respond with humility. It's a way of saying to God, unless you show me your mercy by directing my path, I have no hope of finding my way. This Jesus Prayer, as it has been called down through the ages, attunes our hearts and minds to listen to him. We get another warning today: *Be on your guard against all [kinds of greed], for one's life does not consist in the abundance of possessions."*

If ever there were a warning for our age, particularly in our North American context, it is this one. Life does not consist in an abundance of possessions. Life consists in the possession of abundance. There are two kinds of people: abundance people and scarcity people. An abundance person is possessed by God. A greedy person is possessed by scarcity.

The story Jesus tells today teaches us that no matter how much a scarcity person can amass, it will never be enough. For an abundance person, no matter how little they have, there is always more than enough. Many wealthy people are ironically scarcity people. They keep adding more because they can never have enough. Many poor people are ironically abundance people. It's why when people visit parts of the developing world they often come back talking about how the people they encountered had very little and yet they were unbelievably generous and extraordinarily happy.

Whoever is possessed by God is in possession of abundance. The great antidote to greed is generosity. In the kingdom of God, the more you give, the more you possess. So wherever in life you feel as though you may not have enough—give more of that away. It will surprise you. It will lead to the abundant life.

The Prayer

Lord Jesus Christ, Son of God, have mercy on me, a sinner.
Lord Jesus Christ, Son of God, have mercy on me, a son/daughter.
Lord Jesus Christ, Son of God, have mercy on me, a saint.

The Question

How about it—abundance person or scarcity person—where do you trend? What is your next step?

Learn to Receive

14

LUKE 12:22–34 | Then Jesus said to his disciples: "Therefore I tell you, do not worry about your life, what you will eat; or about your body, what you will wear. For life is more than food, and the body more than clothes. Consider the ravens: They do not sow or reap, they have no storeroom or barn; yet God feeds them. And how much more valuable you are than birds! Who of you by worrying can add a single hour to your life? Since you cannot do this very little thing, why do you worry about the rest?

"Consider how the wild flowers grow. They do not labor or spin. Yet I tell you, not even Solomon in all his splendor was dressed like one of these. If that is how God clothes the grass of the field, which is here today, and tomorrow is thrown into the fire, how much more will he clothe you—you of little faith! And do not set your heart on what you will eat or drink; do not worry about it. For the pagan world runs after all such things, and your Father knows that you need them. But seek his kingdom, and these things will be given to you as well.

"Do not be afraid, little flock, for your Father has been pleased to give you the kingdom. Sell your possessions and give to the poor. Provide purses for yourselves that will not wear out, a treasure in heaven that will never fail, where no thief comes near and no moth destroys. For where your treasure is, there your heart will be also."

Consider This

When I feed the birds, I have never once thought of expecting anything in return. I've got a pretty good hunch that the birds have never thought about paying me back either. Yet by giving freely to them, I receive almost effortlessly from them. I enjoy the glory of their presence and their color and their song. Are they doing that for me? Heavens no! That is just who they are. They are being who they were created to be.

When I plant a flower garden, I don't think about those flowers owing me anything, yet they give to me in ways I could never reciprocate. These flowers are not blooming for me but for the glory of it all. I have no claim on them yet I get to enjoy them.

What if my life could be this way? What if I could freely receive and freely give? When Jesus says, "Seek the kingdom," I think he is saying, "Learn to receive." Here's what I think: to the extent we can receive from God, our lives will be a gift to others. Doesn't Jesus say as much?

"Do not be afraid, little flock, for your Father has been pleased to give you the kingdom. Sell your possessions and give to the poor. Provide purses for yourselves that will not wear out, a treasure in heaven that will never fail, where no thief comes near and no moth destroys. For where your treasure is, there your heart will be also."

The fundamental brokenness of the human race, the essence of the brokenness that we call sin, is the inability to freely receive. Isn't that the story of Eden—we preferred to take (i.e., steal) rather than receive? Fear and anxiety lead to taking. Faith and love lead to receiving.

I'm beginning to think the secret to being a generous person is the ability to freely receive. What if my ability to give is only limited by my ability to receive?

The Prayer

Lord Jesus Christ, Son of God, have mercy on me, a sinner.
Lord Jesus Christ, Son of God, have mercy on me, a
  son/daughter.
Lord Jesus Christ, Son of God, have mercy on me, a saint.

The Question

On a scale of 1–10 (10 is highest), rate your ability to freely receive. What is behind that number? How might you grow this muscle in your soul?

Don't Be Afraid— Be Prepared

15

LUKE 12:35–48 | "Be dressed ready for service and keep your lamps burning, like servants waiting for their master to return from a wedding banquet, so that when he comes and knocks they can immediately open the door for him. It will be good for those servants whose master finds them watching when he comes. Truly I tell you, he will dress himself to serve, will have them recline at the table and will come and wait on them. It will be good for those servants whose master finds them ready, even if he comes in the middle of the night or toward daybreak. But understand this: If the owner of the house had known at what hour the thief was coming, he would not have let his house be broken into. You also must be ready, because the Son of Man will come at an hour when you do not expect him."

Peter asked, "Lord, are you telling this parable to us, or to everyone?"

The Lord answered, "Who then is the faithful and wise manager, whom the master puts in charge of his servants to give them their food allowance at the proper time? It will be good for that servant whom the master finds doing so when he returns. Truly I tell you, he will put him in charge of all his possessions. But suppose the servant says to himself, 'My master is taking a long time in coming,' and he then begins to beat the other servants, both men and women, and to eat and drink and get drunk. The master of that servant will come on a day when he does not expect him and at an hour he is not aware of. He will cut him to pieces and assign him a place with the unbelievers.

"The servant who knows the master's will and does not get ready or does not do what the master wants will be beaten with many blows. But the one who does not know and does things deserving punishment will be beaten with few blows. From everyone who has been given much, much will be demanded;

and from the one who has been entrusted with much, much more will be asked."

Consider This

Today's text continues this series of warnings. We began with the warning against the influence of the Pharisees: hypocrisy. Next Jesus warned about the pursuit of possessions and then about the anxiety that comes from the fear of poverty.

In every case, Jesus makes sweeping contrasts with the way the world works and thinks and the way the kingdom of heaven works. The world operates from a place of scarcity while the kingdom works from a place of abundance.

Jesus has inaugurated the era of the mercy of God, the time in which repentance and reorientation of one's life are not only possible but empowered. The kingdom of God is now breaking in upon the broken world order. Repentance is about getting on board. Jesus reveals what life looks like in the world of God's highest intentions. In these texts we are witnessing him teaching and training people to do this.

Today Jesus puts his teaching into a much larger framework: the end of time and the final consummation of the kingdom. The time will come when all the wrongs will be righted, when justice will finally be served and evil eradicated. Jesus teaches his followers and anyone who would listen not to be afraid but to be prepared. There is an urgency to all of this. This is not a self-improvement program.

We are moving into the heart of the season of Lent now. One of two things can happen at this point. We can grow in our focus or we can get lost in the middle. The middle is like a minefield laden with a thousand trip wires in the form of distractions. It's time to up our attention game. I can't stress it enough. One of the key ways of focusing attention is through an unrelenting obsession with these words. If I were your doctor, and I'm not, I would write you a prescription to say this prayer one hundred times a day.

Lord Jesus Christ, Son of God, have mercy on me, a sinner.

The Prayer
Lord Jesus Christ, Son of God, have mercy on me, a sinner.
Lord Jesus Christ, Son of God, have mercy on me, a son/daughter.
Lord Jesus Christ, Son of God, have mercy on me, a saint.

The Question
When it comes to the return of Jesus and the end of the age, are you more afraid or more prepared or somewhere in between, which unfortunately trends toward ambivalence?

16 Is Your House on Fire?

LUKE 12:49–59 | "I have come to bring fire on the earth, and how I wish it were already kindled! But I have a baptism to undergo, and what constraint I am under until it is completed! Do you think I came to bring peace on earth? No, I tell you, but division. From now on there will be five in one family divided against each other, three against two and two against three. They will be divided, father against son and son against father, mother against daughter and daughter against mother, mother-in-law against daughter-in-law and daughter-in-law against mother-in-law."

He said to the crowd: "When you see a cloud rising in the west, immediately you say, 'It's going to rain,' and it does. And when the south wind blows, you say, 'It's going to be hot,' and it is. Hypocrites! You know how to interpret the appearance of the earth and the sky. How is it that you don't know how to interpret this present time?

"Why don't you judge for yourselves what is right? As you are going with your adversary to the magistrate, try hard to be reconciled on the way, or your adversary may drag you off to the judge, and the judge turn you over to the officer, and the officer throw you into prison. I tell you, you will not get out until you have paid the last penny."

Consider This

Hang on. Did Jesus just say, *"Do you think I came to bring peace on earth? No, I tell you, but division."*

When the Bible seems to say something contradictory, rather than question its integrity or veracity, we must dig for a deeper understanding.

Let's go back to the beginning of Luke's gospel. Remember the night when Jesus was born and the angels appeared to the shepherds? Remember what they were declaring? "Glory to God in the highest heaven, and on earth peace to those on whom his favor rests" (2:14).

Do you remember what happened a bit later after Jesus was born? His parents took him to the temple to be consecrated and they met up with Simeon, who prophesied over them and gave Mary this warning: "This child is destined to cause the falling and rising of many in Israel, and to be a sign that will be spoken against, so that the thoughts of many hearts will be revealed. And a sword will pierce your own soul too" (2:34–35).

Within the span of fifteen verses we go from Jesus as a sign of peace on Earth to Jesus as one who will bring division. It gives us a bigger context for our work of listening to him when he says things like, *Do you think I came to bring peace on earth? No, I tell you, but division.*

Jesus has not come to do a few mission projects on earth—to show us a better way. He has come to inaugurate the kingdom of heaven, and in the process, to reveal the nature of the King of this kingdom. He is bringing the mercy of a preemptive judgment. In other words, he offers anyone and everyone the present opportunity to behold the signs of the in-breaking kingdom of God, and through this, to understand the true nature and character of God. As a result of this, Jesus offers us a free yet urgent invitation to respond by turning away from our misguided ideas about who God is and what God wants and to follow him.

It is our misguided notions of who God is and what God is like that wreaks havoc on the world. A hypocrite, in Luke's understanding, is not a fake. A hypocrite is a person who orders their life around a false idea of who God is. This is why the Pharisees don't repent. They are convinced in the rightness of their understanding and way of life. This is why often the so-called believers are far more dangerous than the unbelievers.

Jesus, by virtue of being who he is, brings division. It's the most merciful thing he can do. People will either respond to him or not. That is the dividing line. Unfortunately, even families will divide over this. The amazing thing is he warns us of what is coming and the urgency of reorienting our lives accordingly. He is not making threats. He is simply telling us the truth. Judgment is coming. We live now in the age of mercy where there is still time.

"I have come to bring fire on the earth, and how I wish it were already kindled!"

It reminds me of an old friend of mine named Ricky. Ricky became a follower of Jesus after a very destructive first half of his life. I remember him telling me of an encounter he had with one of his old friends from that old life. He approached this friend and said, "If I was driving past your house and saw that it was on fire, would you want me to tell you?" The friend responded, "Of course!" Ricky replied, "Okay then, your house is on fire," and proceeded to share the gospel with him. Some might call that confrontational. I think Jesus would call it compassionate.

Wake up out there! Things are heating up. Lent can't be just another lap around the liturgical track. It is a holy opportunity for realignment. Let's pay attention. Let's listen to him.

The Prayer

Lord Jesus Christ, Son of God, have mercy on me, a sinner.
Lord Jesus Christ, Son of God, have mercy on me, a son/daughter.
Lord Jesus Christ, Son of God, have mercy on me, a saint.

The Question

How do you relate to this notion of the merciful divisiveness of Jesus?

Third Sunday of Lent

Don't "Behave." Become!

LUKE 13:1–9 | Now there were some present at that time who told Jesus about the Galileans whose blood Pilate had mixed with their sacrifices. Jesus answered, "Do you think that these Galileans were worse sinners than all the other Galileans because they suffered this way? I tell you, no! But unless you repent, you too will all perish. Or those eighteen who died when the tower in Siloam fell on them—do you think they were more guilty than all the others living in Jerusalem? I tell you, no! But unless you repent, you too will all perish."

Then he told this parable: "A man had a fig tree growing in his vineyard, and he went to look for fruit on it but did not find any. So he said to the man who took care of the vineyard, 'For three years now I've been coming to look for fruit on this fig tree and haven't found any. Cut it down! Why should it use up the soil?'

"'Sir,' the man replied, 'leave it alone for one more year, and I'll dig around it and fertilize it. If it bears fruit next year, fine! If not, then cut it down.'"

Consider This

I will never forget the Sunday following the Monday of August 29, 2005. It was the Sunday after the Monday on which occurred the most devastating and deadly natural disaster in the history of the United States: Hurricane Katrina.

I remember it because of what the preacher said in the church I visited that Sunday. To sum up one of the worst sermons I ever heard in my forty-eight years of hearing sermons, he said this: "Hurricane Katrina was God's judgment on the people and city of New Orleans, Louisiana." And he got more than a few amens.

Underneath this message is a completely wrong notion of who God is and what God is like. Bad things happen to bad people. Translation: the reason Hurricane Katrina did not destroy our town (besides the convenient fact that we were living a thousand miles inland) is because we were living lives that please God.

That's what's going on in today's text. In the midst of Jesus' message to the crowds about the judgment of God, someone interrupts him with this kind of query. In essence, they were saying, "Oh, we get it. It's like that time when Pilate slaughtered those Galileans at the temple as they were coming to offer their sacrifices. They had it coming, didn't they? They were being judged by God." Hiding just beneath the surface of their theological pronouncement was their self-assured sense of righteousness that prevented such a thing from happening to them.

Let's just say Jesus swung for the fence on that one. Check it out again.

"Do you think that these Galileans were worse sinners than all the other Galileans because they suffered this way? I tell

you, no! But unless you repent, you too will all perish. Or those eighteen who died when the tower in Siloam fell on them—do you think they were more guilty than all the others living in Jerusalem? I tell you, no! But unless you repent, you too will all perish."

I want you to notice the placement of the exclamation point in the passage above. To their tragedy he adds one of his own: the falling of the tower in Siloam. He might as well have said Hurricane Katrina. Jesus effectively says no one will be immune from divine judgment. Neither does the judgment of God happen by falling towers and senseless tragedies. The judgment of God is a given, or else there is no ultimate justice and if there is no ultimate justice there can be no ultimate mercy either.

The kingdom of God is the world made right again. To repent is to join that movement. But it's time to reframe repentance. For too long we've primarily associated repentance with someone pointing a finger at us and saying, "Behave!" Here's how I see it. Repentance is the hand of Jesus reaching out to us with the invitation to "become." Becoming begins with beholding God as he truly is (i.e., like Jesus). When a person catches a glimpse of the true and living God and they begin to really believe, they also begin to believe in the possibility of their life becoming far more than they ever imagined before. Anyone who has walked more than a mile or two down this road knows that behavior has a way of taking care of itself when the Holy Spirit–empowered process of becoming takes root.

Speaking of roots, isn't that what Jesus is getting at in the parable he told them?

"A man had a fig tree growing in his vineyard, and he went to look for fruit on it but did not find any. So he said to the man who took care of the vineyard, 'For three years now I've been coming to look for fruit on this fig tree and haven't found any. Cut it down! Why should it use up the soil?'"

The man wants to bring judgment on the tree for failing to bear fruit. Not so fast, Jesus says.

"'Sir,' the man replied, 'leave it alone for one more year, and I'll dig around it and fertilize it. If it bears fruit next year, fine! If not, then cut it down.'"

God, in his mercy, is holding back. To repent means to be rooted in the life of God in order to become the person God dreamed you to be in the first place. Listen to how Peter puts it in his letter:

> The Lord is not slow to fulfill his promise as some count slowness, but is patient toward you, not wishing that any should perish, but that all should reach repentance. (2 Peter 3:9 ESV)

Repentance is not about behaving but rather a beautiful, humble way of life—a glorious life. It's getting on board with the only kingdom that will stand forever.

The Prayer
Lord Jesus Christ, Son of God, have mercy on me, a sinner.

*Lord Jesus Christ, Son of God, have mercy on me, a
    son/daughter.*
Lord Jesus Christ, Son of God, have mercy on me, a saint.

The Question

Is your vision of repentance still more shaped by behavior management or by a becoming process? How do you see the difference?

Let Your Life Teach 17

LUKE 13:10–17 | On a Sabbath Jesus was teaching in one of the synagogues, and a woman was there who had been crippled by a spirit for eighteen years. She was bent over and could not straighten up at all. When Jesus saw her, he called her forward and said to her, "Woman, you are set free from your infirmity." Then he put his hands on her, and immediately she straightened up and praised God. Indignant because Jesus had healed on the Sabbath, the synagogue leader said to the people, "There are six days for work. So come and be healed on those days, not on the Sabbath." The Lord answered him, "You hypocrites! Doesn't each of you on the Sabbath untie your ox or donkey from the stall and lead it out to give it water? Then should not this woman, a daughter of Abraham, whom Satan has kept bound for eighteen long years, be set free on the Sabbath day from what bound her?" When he said this, all his opponents were humiliated, but the people were delighted with all the wonderful things he was doing.

Consider This

So first I want you to count the number of times the word *Sabbath* is repeated in the passage above. There's a point being made here.

Now take note of the scene unfolding here and the cast. Jesus is up front teaching. There's a woman who is physically deformed. There's the synagogue leader, and finally, the crowd. Though they are not explicitly mentioned, we can be sure his disciples were present, which brings me to my next point.

Something we all too easily forget is the big picture of what is constantly happening in the gospel accounts. Jesus is making disciples. The overwhelming way we tend to read the Gospels is through the lens of salvation, and rightfully so. What if the Gospels are also meant to serve as Jesus' discipleship manual? What if Jesus actually intends to disciple us through our reading of the Gospels? Isn't that what the big idea of the Father telling us to listen to him on Transfiguration Mountain is all about?

Jesus, by the power of the Holy Spirit, disciples us directly through our close and careful engagement with the gospel accounts.

Back to the scene at hand. Luke, a medical doctor no less, presents us with an impossible situation—one no doctor could solve. This woman had been bent over from the waist down for over eighteen years. Note Luke's diagnosis: crippled by a spirit. What this tells us is the woman was a person of no status. She would have been regarded as a lost and worthless person who was probably getting what she deserved. She would have been virtually invisible to the society around her.

Here comes the discipleship lesson for the day: *When Jesus saw her . . .*

Truth is, if Jesus hadn't seen her we would probably not be talking about her. She would not have been mentioned. Jesus is actually creating an unforgettable moment here. Whatever Jesus was teaching at the time, he just changed the lesson plan.

He called her forward and said to her . . .

Jesus brought this unnamed woman of no status to the very front of the room—to the place of honor. He exalts the humble.

"Woman, you are set free from your infirmity." Then he put his hands on her, and immediately she straightened up and praised God.

Remember that early synagogue scene in Nazareth, the one where he read from Isaiah 61 about the captives being set free and the poor hearing good news and the oppressed being released? You remember this. It was when Jesus rolled up the ancient scroll, sat down, and spoke the sentence heard round the world: "Today, this scripture is fulfilled in your hearing." Well, that scene back there is this scene in action. Now the fireworks start going off.

*Indignant because Jesus had healed on the Sabbath, the syna-
gogue leader said to the people, "There are six days for work. So
come and be healed on those days, not on the Sabbath."*

This is a shame tactic. The synagogue leader was trying
to humiliate Jesus. This is the part where Jesus humbles the
exalted.

*The Lord answered him, "You hypocrites! Doesn't each of you
on the Sabbath untie your ox or donkey from the stall and lead
it out to give it water? Then should not this woman, a daughter
of Abraham, whom Satan has kept bound for eighteen long
years, be set free on the Sabbath day from what bound her?"*

Let's just say Jesus gave him the smackdown. There's so
much more to say about this, but I've got to close.

I think the final point I'd like to make relates back to the
point on how Jesus makes disciples. We have no idea what
Jesus was teaching that day as he stood in the front of the
synagogue. There is a massive lesson afoot here in the form
of a conflict over how to interpret the Bible. It's the same
battle we saw between Jesus and Satan earlier in the wilderness. The big difference? Jesus becomes his interpretation. He
is the Word made flesh. This is the big lesson for disciples
and disciple makers. They may not remember what you said,
but they will never forget what you did. Your life is the lesson.

The Prayer
Lord Jesus Christ, Son of God, have mercy on me, a sinner.
*Lord Jesus Christ, Son of God, have mercy on me, a
    son/daughter.*
Lord Jesus Christ, Son of God, have mercy on me, a saint.

The Question

Sometimes you can be right and still be wrong. Ever seen a situation like that? Been in one?

Believe Big in the Power of Small

18

LUKE 13:18–30 ESV | He said therefore, "What is the kingdom of God like? And to what shall I compare it? It is like a grain of mustard seed that a man took and sowed in his garden, and it grew and became a tree, and the birds of the air made nests in its branches."

And again he said, "To what shall I compare the kingdom of God? It is like leaven that a woman took and hid in three measures of flour, until it was all leavened."

He went on his way through towns and villages, teaching and journeying toward Jerusalem. And someone said to him, "Lord, will those who are saved be few?" And he said to them, "Strive to enter through the narrow door. For many, I tell you, will seek to enter and will not be able. When once the master of the house has risen and shut the door, and you begin to stand outside and to knock at the door, saying, 'Lord, open to us,' then he will answer you, 'I do not know where you come from.' Then you will begin to say, 'We ate and drank in your presence, and you taught in our streets.' But he will say, 'I tell you, I do not know where you come from. Depart from me, all you workers of evil!' In that place there will be weeping and gnashing of teeth, when you see Abraham and Isaac and Jacob and all the prophets in the kingdom of God but you yourselves cast out. And people will come from east and west, and from north and south, and recline at table in the kingdom of God. And behold, some are last who will be first, and some are first who will be last."

Consider This

A few observations about these two parables that open our reading for today:

1. Seeds contain inestimable possibilities.

2. Jesus' big point is that a tiny seed is capable of producing something far greater than itself—in this case a great tree.

3. Seeds also reproduce themselves exponentially. Conservatively speaking, one seed of wheat will produce on average 200 seeds of wheat; 200 seeds of wheat will produce on average 40,000 seeds of wheat; 40,000 seeds of wheat will produce on average 8,000,000 seeds of wheat; 8,000,000 seeds of wheat will produce on average 1,600,000,000 seeds of wheat.

4. Approximate number of Christians in the world today: 2,000,000,000. Number of seeds at the beginning: 1. See also John 12:24.

5. To further demonstrate the nature of the kingdom of God, Jesus takes us into the domain of a woman in the first century, her kitchen. That's way out of the box for the first century to even make such an absurd analogy.

6. Like the mustard seed, yeast has power far dispropor-
tionate to its size. In this case, the tiny bit of yeast works
through sixty pounds of flour, making enough bread to feed
hundreds of people.

The gospel of the kingdom is extraordinary, extravagant,
and it excels beyond our wildest imagination. That's why
Paul would later say things like this:

> Now to him who is able to do immeasurably more
> than all we ask or imagine, according to his power that
> is at work within us, to him be glory in the church and
> in Christ Jesus throughout all generations, for ever and
> ever! Amen. (Eph. 3:20–21)

Later Jesus will tell us when our faith is anchored in a
gospel like this, it only takes faith the size of a mustard seed
itself. We need mercy to have even a smidgen of the capacity
it takes to fathom such possibilities as these.

The Prayer

Lord Jesus Christ, Son of God, have mercy on me, a sinner.
Lord Jesus Christ, Son of God, have mercy on me, a
   son/daughter.
Lord Jesus Christ, Son of God, have mercy on me, a saint.

The Question

What would it mean for you to see and understand yourself as a sower of the kingdom of God? Today?

19 Surrender to God— Don't Resign to Circumstance

LUKE 13:31–35 | At that time some Pharisees came to Jesus and said to him, "Leave this place and go somewhere else. Herod wants to kill you."

He replied, "Go tell that fox, 'I will keep on driving out demons and healing people today and tomorrow, and on the third day I will reach my goal.' In any case, I must press on today and tomorrow and the next day—for surely no prophet can die outside Jerusalem!

"Jerusalem, Jerusalem, you who kill the prophets and stone those sent to you, how often I have longed to gather your children together, as a hen gathers her chicks under her wings, and you were not willing. Look, your house is left to you desolate. I tell you, you will not see me again until you say, 'Blessed is he who comes in the name of the Lord.'"

Consider This

We learn something incredibly important from listening to Jesus in today's text. It's subtle, but it can make all the difference, especially in hard times.

Jesus knows the inevitable outcome that awaits him in Jerusalem. He has spoken explicitly about it to his disciples since coming down from Transfiguration Mountain. He knows he faces an awful ordeal on the horizon.

Rather than accepting the inevitable future, he abandons himself to God. Jesus is defiant in the face of death because he is secure in the hands of his Father. He knows there will be a third day on the other side of the cross. He knew he was held by the kind of power that never fails, that never gives up, that always protects, always trusts, always hopes, always perseveres. In short, he knew because he was held by the power of Love that he could love powerfully all the way to the end and beyond.

One of my favorite Charles Wesley hymn lyrics comes in the third verse of the great apostolic anthem, "And Can It Be."

> *He left his Father's throne above (so free, so infinite his grace!),*
> *Emptied himself of all but love and bled for Adam's help-less race.*

This is the goal of we who follow him and as we abandon ourselves to him, he will accomplish it in and through us. This is the great secret to the crisis and process of sanctification (the Bible word for becoming like Jesus): to empty ourselves of all but love. He bled so we could become. Life's hardest experiences offer the opportunities for love's greatest exploits—come what may.

I witnessed an of aspect of discipleship from my friend and mentor, Maxie Dunnam, when I served under his leadership at Asbury Seminary. We were going through an extremely challenging season at the seminary owing to the devastating impact of the post-Enron economic collapse on the strength of the school's endowment. It was creating tremendous stress and strain on a lot of people and chiefly on Dr. Dunnam, who was the president of the school.

I remember him sharing with me a word of wisdom he had received from the Lord in the midst of it all. He put it this way: "God is teaching me the difference between a spirit of resignation to the situation and an intentional act of surrender to God." This word encouraged him to resolve himself to a deeper consecration to God in the face of the challenge rather than resigning himself to the apparent inevitabilities of a situation out of his control. Those were difficult days, and we have the scars to prove it, but God brought us through and made us better in the process.

Let me close with a word of encouragement. Whatever you may be facing—a diagnosis of cancer, a crumbling marriage, financial ruin, prodigal sons or daughters, the pain of rejection, a very uncertain future—don't resign yourself to some inevitable outcome. At the same time, reject mere optimism and renounce pessimism. Surrender to the inevitability of the undefeatable love of God. Abandon yourself to Jesus, the One who has abandoned himself for you.

The Prayer

Lord Jesus Christ, Son of God, have mercy on me, a sinner.
Lord Jesus Christ, Son of God, have mercy on me, a
   son/daughter.
Lord Jesus Christ, Son of God, have mercy on me, a saint.

The Question

How do you see the difference between a spirit of resignation to a circumstance and an intentioned surrender to God in the midst of it? Remember a time like that?

Be a Shield, Not a Sword

20

LUKE 14:1–6 | One Sabbath, when Jesus went to eat in the house of a prominent Pharisee, he was being carefully watched. There in front of him was a man suffering from abnormal swelling of his body. Jesus asked the Pharisees and experts in the law, "Is it lawful to heal on the Sabbath or not?" But they remained silent. So taking hold of the man, he healed him and sent him on his way.

Then he asked them, "If one of you has a child or an ox that falls into a well on the Sabbath day, will you not immediately pull it out?" And they had nothing to say.

Consider This

One of the enduring lessons I learned from my legal education has to do with the nature of law and its purpose in life.

I remember the way one of my law professors put it. The law intends to serve as a shield to protect people, but lawyers will readily use the law as a sword to pierce them.

We see it at work in today's text. By now, the Sabbath has become a major flash point in the battle being waged by the Pharisees against Jesus. It's gotten to the point that they invite him into their homes on the Sabbath in order to further prosecute him. Note the text tells us Jesus was being "carefully watched."

These Pharisees and legal experts wielded the law as a sword. They were out to pierce Jesus, to cut him to pieces. (Their strategy will ultimately succeed.) Jesus constantly lifts our eyes to the higher aims of the law. He never sets the law aside, rather he fulfills it by living into its greater purpose— that of protecting and preserving the humanity of people.

In today's text the classic confrontation is on again. A man suffering with an awful disease stands before Jesus. How he got there we have no idea, but we can be sure he was not invited. Jesus sees before him a broken image-bearer of the Most High God, a priceless son of Adam.

Jesus asked the Pharisees and experts in the law, "Is it lawful to heal on the Sabbath or not?" But they remained silent. So taking hold of the man, he healed him and sent him on his way.

The law, Jesus says, is a shield of protection, a place of refuge; indeed, it is intended to reestablish the norms of the very garden of Eden. Unless we understand it in this way, we are doomed to a never-ending game of gotcha. Jesus presses it further:

Then he asked them, "If one of you has a child or an ox that falls into a well on the Sabbath day, will you not immediately pull it out?" And they had nothing to say.

Jesus seems to be systematically going to all the people who have been devastated by the Pharisees' sword-like application of the law. There's major learning to be had here. I will put it bluntly.

To the extent we don't see and love the broken and hurting and lost among us, we don't see and love God. To that extent our religion is little more than a policy manual. To the extent our hearts are hardened toward the poor, they are hardened toward God. Didn't one of the Proverbs say something like this? "Those who mock the poor insult their Maker" (Prov. 17:5, author's paraphrase). In the final analysis, he will say, "As you have done it unto the least of these you have done it unto me" (Matt. 25:40, author's paraphrase).

So how about you? Are you a shield person or a sword person? This has nothing to do with whether you are a rule follower or not. It's whether or not you are a follower of the Ruler.

The Prayer

Lord Jesus Christ, Son of God, have mercy on me, a sinner.
Lord Jesus Christ, Son of God, have mercy on me, a
    son/daughter.
Lord Jesus Christ, Son of God, have mercy on me, a saint.

The Question

There are the rules, and there is the Spirit of the Ruler. Where do you tend to focus your energies? See the difference?

21 Seek Relationship with People in Need

LUKE 14:7–24 | When he noticed how the guests picked the places of honor at the table, he told them this parable: "When someone invites you to a wedding feast, do not take the place of honor, for a person more distinguished than you may have been invited. If so, the host who invited both of you will come and say to you, 'Give this person your seat.' Then, humiliated, you will have to take the least important place. But when you are invited, take the lowest place, so that when your host comes, he will say to you, 'Friend, move up to a better place.' Then you will be honored in the presence of all the other guests. For all those who exalt themselves will be humbled, and those who humble themselves will be exalted."

Then Jesus said to his host, "When you give a luncheon or dinner, do not invite your friends, your brothers or sisters, your relatives, or your rich neighbors; if you do, they may invite you back and so you will be repaid. But when you give a banquet, invite the poor, the crippled, the lame, the blind, and you will be blessed. Although they cannot repay you, you will be repaid at the resurrection of the righteous."

When one of those at the table with him heard this, he said to Jesus, "Blessed is the one who will eat at the feast in the kingdom of God."

Jesus replied: "A certain man was preparing a great banquet and invited many guests. At the time of the banquet he sent his servant to tell those who had been invited, 'Come, for everything is now ready.'"

But they all alike began to make excuses. The first said, 'I have just bought a field, and I must go and see it. Please excuse me.'

"Another said, 'I have just bought five yoke of oxen, and I'm on my way to try them out. Please excuse me.'

"Still another said, 'I just got married, so I can't come.'

"The servant came back and reported this to his master. Then the owner of the house became angry and ordered his servant, 'Go out quickly into the streets and alleys of the town and bring in the poor, the crippled, the blind and the lame.'

"'Sir,' the servant said, 'what you ordered has been done, but there is still room.'

"Then the master told his servant, 'Go out to the roads and country lanes and compel them to come in, so that my house will be full. I tell you, not one of those who were invited will get a taste of my banquet.'"

Consider This

The poor, the crippled, the blind, and the lame.

I have no idea what it is like to be any of these people.

I do know what it is like to be rich (in comparison to the majority of people in the world). I know what is like to be healthy, independent, privileged, and honored.

Jesus clearly favored the down-and-out. Why is this?

Perhaps it is because these were the people who knew their need of God. That's the dangerous thing about wealth and health and security and independence and privilege and honor; they insulate us from staying in touch with our need of God.

We need to remember, Jesus is having dinner with people of status and honor. These remarks are addressed to them. He is telling people of privilege (like me and probably you) what following him looks like for them.

"When someone invites you to a wedding feast, do not take the place of honor, . . . But when you are invited, take the lowest place. . . . But when you give a banquet, invite the poor, the crippled, the lame, the blind, and you will be blessed."

Jesus is teaching us what God is like, and it is surprising. We tend to live by the old adage, often attributed to the Bible, "The Lord helps those who help themselves." According to Jesus, this could not be further from the truth. Jesus seems to say, "The Lord helps those who cannot help themselves." He tells us, in effect, if we want to be like God (i.e., holy), we must seek out these people who cannot help themselves. Why?

This is not charity he's talking about. It's not a handout he's asking for. Jesus is calling us to invite them to our banquet— to treat them as our friends, to enter into relationship with them. Why?

The closer we get to these people who cannot help them-selves, the more we will realize they are fundamentally the same as us. The closer we get to them, the less we will be able to hide behind our theory that they are getting what they deserve; which is another way of saying we are getting what we deserve. The more we come into touch with people in need of mercy, the more in touch we will become of our own need for mercy because we will come to realize that just as no person deserves to be poor, no person deserves to be rich either. At the core of the core, we are the same.

Jesus isn't after a permanent welfare state any more than he is for the forced redistribution of wealth. Jesus is looking for the love of God to become the core and compelling reality of our lives. This love makes us humble and helpful, which is another way of saying holy.

The truth? The rich are in need of the poor as much or more than the poor are in need of the rich. It's not about charitable giving and the transfer of wealth. It's about what money can never buy: human relationships founded in the love of God.

The Prayer

Lord Jesus Christ, Son of God, have mercy on me, a sinner.
Lord Jesus Christ, Son of God, have mercy on me, a
   son/daughter.
Lord Jesus Christ, Son of God, have mercy on me, a saint.

The Question

Why do we tend to subscribe to the belief and value system that people get what they deserve? How tightly do you cling to this? What would it cost to let it go?

22 Conjunction Junction: AND or OR?

LUKE 14:25–35 | Large crowds were traveling with Jesus, and turning to them he said: "If anyone comes to me and does not hate father and mother, wife and children, brothers and sisters—yes, even their own life—such a person cannot be my disciple. And whoever does not carry their cross and follow me cannot be my disciple.

"Suppose one of you wants to build a tower. Won't you first sit down and estimate the cost to see if you have enough money to complete it? For if you lay the foundation and are not able to finish it, everyone who sees it will ridicule you, saying, 'This person began to build and wasn't able to finish.'

"Or suppose a king is about to go to war against another king. Won't he first sit down and consider whether he is able with ten thousand men to oppose the one coming against him with twenty thousand? If he is not able, he will send a delegation while the other is still a long way off and will ask for terms of peace. In the same way, those of you who do not give up everything you have cannot be my disciples.

"Salt is good, but if it loses its saltiness, how can it be made salty again? It is fit neither for the soil nor for the manure pile; it is thrown out.

"Whoever has ears to hear, let them hear."

Consider This

He's clearly gone too far this time. What's this about having to hate my mom and dad and sisters and even my life in order to be a disciple of Jesus? Is he serious?

Yes, he's dead serious, only we must understand what he means by hate. He does not mean hate as in, "I despise you," or as in, "You are dead to me." It's not an affective term at all. He's talking about the priority of one's allegiances and loyalties.

Let's remember what this journey to Jerusalem is all about. Jesus is making disciples. He's teaching and demonstrating what it means to follow him into the kingdom of God, the ever-present and everlasting reality of eternal life.

Let's recapture our bearings. Our journey to Jerusalem is bookended by two similar things Jesus said to his disciples, first in Luke 9 and again in Luke 18:

> "Let these words sink into your ears: The Son of Man is about to be delivered into the hands of men." But they did not understand this saying, and it was concealed from them, so that they might not perceive it. And they were afraid to ask him about this saying. (9:44–45 ESV)

> And taking the twelve, he said to them, "See, we are going up to Jerusalem, and everything that is written about the Son of Man by the prophets will be accomplished. For he will be delivered over to the Gentiles and will be mocked and shamefully treated and spit upon. And after flogging him, they will kill him, and on the third day he will rise."

> But they understood none of these things. This saying
> was hidden from them, and they did not grasp what was
> said. (18:31–34 ESV)

Most interesting here (at least to me) is the similarity in the last sentence in each passage. We find ourselves, with the disciples, somewhere in the middle of these two bookended sayings. This land in-between is the land of *listening to him*, the territory of transformation, the path of discipleship. It's also a place that can be challenging to understand.

In today's text, Jesus is working to separate the wheat from the chaff, the crowds from the converts. He isn't breaking up families. He's clarifying allegiances. He's effectively saying, "When the time comes and a conflict emerges between your family's values and the way of my kingdom, your choice needs to have already been made. Count the cost now."

Looking back, he's made this abundantly clear with respect to wealth, status, prestige, and honor. To the extent our trust in wealth conflicts with our trust in him, our wealth is a problem. In such a case we don't have wealth; our wealth has us. Same with family. Family is a great gift of God, but to the extent our family impedes our discipleship it's a problem. Jesus is not giving us ultimatums and either-ors. He's calling for steadfast, singular allegiance. In fact, he basically says if you place your only allegiance and trust in me, then the rest of your life, your family and wealth and relationships and so forth, will come into order. If you try and split your allegiances and hedge your bets, in the end you will have neither me nor those things you trusted in.

Bottom line: following Jesus comes down to all-in or not in at all. I don't want it to be that way. I want to soften this for reasonable people, and the church I have grown up in so far has done just this. Maybe that's why the church I've grown up in looks more like the crowds than the disciples.

We want the ease of the and. You can follow Jesus *and* pursue great wealth. You can follow Jesus *and* make your family your own little island kingdom. You can follow Jesus *and* live in the self-assured status of your social importance. The truth? Jesus is not about the and, but the or. The power is in the or. He's calling for a decisive choice to be all-in with him. The power of the or is the way it leads to real abundance. It's not Jesus *or* family. It's just Jesus. It's not Jesus *or* wealth. It's just Jesus. It's not Jesus *or* status, prestige, and power. It's just Jesus.

And Jesus has a marvelous way he brings the and back around for those who choose the or. "Seek first his kingdom and his righteousness," he said, "*and* all these things will be added to you" (Matt. 6:33, emphasis added).

Let me close with another of Jesus' sayings we will do well to listen to. Back in chapter 9 Peter made his famous confession of Jesus as the Messiah. If that were to happen in today's church, we would slap high fives and do chest bumps and rush off to baptism and a great lunch. Then we would try to get them involved in the crowd—I mean church activities.

Not Jesus. Immediately on the heels of this earth-shaking confession, he says this: "For whoever wants to save their life will lose it, but whoever loses their life for me will save it" (Luke 9:24).

It's time we love people enough to invite them into this kind of life-losing/life-saving life. Until we do, we are just playing the crowd, I mean church.

All who will go all-in for Jesus will find him becoming all-in-all for us. There's no better place on earth.

The Prayer

Lord Jesus Christ, Son of God, have mercy on me, a sinner.
Lord Jesus Christ, Son of God, have mercy on me, a
  son/daughter.
Lord Jesus Christ, Son of God, have mercy on me, a saint.

The Question

What might it mean for you to become less of an and person and more of an or person? Not Jesus and, but Jesus or.

Fourth Sunday of Lent

Don't Settle to Be a Servant

LUKE 15:1–32 ESV | Now the tax collectors and sinners were all drawing near to hear him. And the Pharisees and the scribes grumbled, saying, "This man receives sinners and eats with them."

So he told them this parable: "What man of you, having a hundred sheep, if he has lost one of them, does not leave the ninety-nine in the open country, and go after the one that is lost, until he finds it? And when he has found it, he lays it on his shoulders, rejoicing. And when he comes home, he calls together his friends and his neighbors, saying to them, 'Rejoice with me, for I have found my sheep that was lost.' Just so, I tell you, there will be more joy in heaven over one sinner who repents than over ninety-nine righteous persons who need no repentance.

"Or what woman, having ten silver coins, if she loses one coin, does not light a lamp and sweep the house and seek diligently until she finds it? And when she has found it, she calls together her friends and neighbors, saying, 'Rejoice with me, for I have found the coin that I had lost.' Just so, I tell you, there is joy before the angels of God over one sinner who repents."

And he said, "There was a man who had two sons. And the younger of them said to his father, 'Father, give me the share of property that is coming to me.' And he divided his property between them. Not many days later, the younger son gathered all he had and took a journey into a far country, and there he squandered his property in reckless living. And when he had spent everything, a severe famine arose in that country, and he began to be in need. So he went and hired himself out to one of the citizens of that country, who sent him into his fields to feed pigs. And he was longing to be fed with the pods that the pigs ate, and no one gave him anything.

"But when he came to himself, he said, 'How many of my father's hired servants have more than enough bread, but I perish here with hunger! I will arise and go to my father, and I will say to him, "Father, I have sinned against heaven and before you. I am no longer worthy to be called your son. Treat me as one of your hired servants."' And he arose and came to his father. But while he was still a long way off, his father saw him and felt compassion, and ran and embraced him and kissed him. And the son said to him, 'Father, I have sinned against heaven and before you. I am no longer worthy to be called your son.' But the father said to his servants, 'Bring quickly the best robe, and put it on him, and put a ring on his hand, and shoes on his feet. And bring the fattened calf and kill it, and let us eat and celebrate. For this my son was dead, and is alive again; he was lost, and is found.' And they began to celebrate.

"Now his older son was in the field, and as he came and drew near to the house, he heard music and dancing. And he called one of the servants and asked what these things meant. And he said to him, 'Your brother has come, and your father has killed the fattened calf, because he has received him back safe and sound.' But he was angry and refused to go in. His father came out and entreated him, but he answered his father, 'Look, these many years I have served you, and I never disobeyed your command, yet you never gave me a young goat, that I might celebrate with my friends. But when this son of yours came, who has devoured your property with prostitutes, you killed the fattened calf for him!' And he said to him, 'Son, you are always with me, and all that is mine is yours. It was fitting to celebrate and be glad, for this your brother was dead, and is alive; he was lost, and is found.'"

Consider This

These stories offer almost endless opportunities and possibilities for learning and reflection. If you think you've "been there and done that and gotten the T-shirt" as relates to chapter 15 of Luke, you can be assured you have not. This is a text for one's whole life. We need to hear that echo from Transfiguration Mountain when the Father told us to listen to him.

Because the text was so lengthy today, I will be brief with the reflection. I want to focus on the short speeches made by the two different sons to their father.

Son #1: "Father, I have sinned against heaven and against you. I am no longer worthy to be called your son; make me like one of your hired servants."

Son #2: "Look! All these years I've been slaving for you and never disobeyed your orders. Yet you never gave me even a young goat so I could celebrate with my friends."

Son #1 knew he was a son though he lived in the Far Country; Son #2 had forgotten he was a son though he lived in his father's house.

Son #1 knew he needed mercy; Son #2 felt he deserved a celebration; he knew nothing about mercy.

Son #1 was willing to forfeit his sonship in order to be a servant; Son #2 actually did forfeit his sonship in order to be a servant.

Son #1 never imagined getting a celebration; Son #2 could not bring himself to go to the party.

Both sons were lost, though only one knew it. Only one son was found.

It's often most difficult for those closest to home to come inside.

We don't have a God who is looking for servants. We have a Father who is in search of sons and daughters.

Don't settle for the servants' quarters. Keep praying . . .

Lord Jesus Christ, Son of God, have mercy on me, a sinner.

The Prayer

Lord Jesus Christ, Son of God, have mercy on me, a sinner.
Lord Jesus Christ, Son of God, have mercy on me, a
   son/daughter.
Lord Jesus Christ, Son of God, have mercy on me, a saint.

The Question
Generally speaking, are you more like the prodigal son or the older brother?

Take a Course in Higher Math

23

LUKE 16:1–12 | Jesus told his disciples: "There was a rich man whose manager was accused of wasting his possessions. So he called him in and asked him, 'What is this I hear about you? Give an account of your management, because you cannot be manager any longer.'

"The manager said to himself, 'What shall I do now? My master is taking away my job. I'm not strong enough to dig, and I'm ashamed to beg—I know what I'll do so that, when I lose my job here, people will welcome me into their houses.'

"So he called in each one of his master's debtors. He asked the first, 'How much do you owe my master?'

"'Nine hundred gallons of olive oil,' he replied.

"The manager told him, 'Take your bill, sit down quickly, and make it four hundred and fifty.'

"Then he asked the second, 'And how much do you owe?'

"'A thousand bushels of wheat,' he replied.

"He told him, 'Take your bill and make it eight hundred.'

"The master commended the dishonest manager because he had acted shrewdly. For the people of this world are more shrewd in dealing with their own kind than are the people of the light. I tell you, use worldly wealth to gain friends for yourselves, so that when it is gone, you will be welcomed into eternal dwellings.

"Whoever can be trusted with very little can also be trusted with much, and whoever is dishonest with very little will also be dishonest with much. So if you have not been trustworthy in handling worldly wealth, who will trust you with true riches? And if you have not been trustworthy with someone else's property, who will give you property of your own?"

Consider This

Our daughter, Lily, spoke a prescient word of wisdom some time ago on the way to school. Seemingly out of the blue, at least to me, she said this, "Da-da, I've been thinking. If Adam and Eve had not eaten the apple then we wouldn't need money, and if we didn't need money we wouldn't need math, and if we didn't need math, the world would be a better place."

Now, getting beyond her obvious distaste for math, the more I think about it the more I think she has something. At least today's text proves her point out in principle. How so?

For starters, note Jesus is setting the parable up in the framework of the present age, which is characterized by the brokenness caused by evil, and the age to come, which is characterized by the kingdom of God, which is already breaking in through his ministry. Jesus' teachings strike us as bewilderingly counterintuitive at times precisely because he is instructing us to live in the present evil age as though the future age of the kingdom of God were already here. In fact, when we live in this fashion, the watching world witnesses something of the good-overcoming-evil presence and power of God in the here and now. Jesus' life offers us an ever-unfolding moving picture of this reality and through the sending of the Holy Spirit, he designs for his life to continue unfolding through the lives of his people. As Jesus was on earth, so we are becoming.

In short, when we live our lives as though the yet-to-come kingdom of God were now afoot in the world, it causes one of two outcomes: People will come to believe in God and enter the kingdom, or they will reject God in favor of the short-lived gains the world has to offer. Discipleship, or following Jesus, is all about learning to live this kind of kingdom of God life in the real world.

It's why we keep on praying, "Lord Jesus Christ, Son of God, have mercy on me, a sinner." Remember, sinner simply names the condition into which we are born; the world gone wrong because unfortunately Adam and Eve ate the apple, to put it in Lily's terms. The greatest danger we face in life is the failure to come to grips with this truth and to turn away from evil and turn to God. The more we make our life work in the present age, the less apt we are to welcome any sort of way of life that works against it.

So what makes our life seemingly work well in this present age? The amassing of power through hoarding wealth, seeking identity in status, honor, and prestige, and worst of all, cloaking our efforts to gain power, wealth, and status in the name of God through public demonstrations of our awesomeness. Summarizing—living a life where everything is driven by the constantly calculating math of self-interest. (This is why soon Jesus will point to a widow and two coins to teach us that generosity is never a matter of how much you give but how much you keep.)

So what does today's text have to do with all of this—in a hundred words or less? Back to the math lesson. Jesus tells us to learn from the shrewd and dishonest manager, who used his master's money to make friends with his master's debtors (also people of great means who could pay him back; i.e., one thousand bushels of wheat, etc.) in order to secure favors from them in his soon-to-be unemployed state.

Jesus teaches us to bank our security not in the present age, which is passing away, but in the age to come, which will never end. We do this by using power, wealth, and status to secretly make friends who can never pay us back; namely, people who don't have power, wealth, and status. It means throwing away the calculator in favor of what I like to call "higher math." It's a math that will never add up in the present age, and yet when people see it at work, their eyes will be lifted to God, because they will have had a preview of the age to come—which in essence is a review of the world as it began (before Adam and Eve ate the apple). This is the world that God is now making.

"If Adam and Eve had not eaten the apple then we wouldn't need money, and if we didn't need money we wouldn't need math, and if we didn't need math, the world would be a better place." Thanks, Lily.

This is hard stuff. Self-interest dies a thousand deaths, but the greatest danger of all is the deception of pride which keeps us from the self-knowledge of our self-interest.

The Prayer

Lord Jesus Christ, Son of God, have mercy on me, a sinner.
Lord Jesus Christ, Son of God, have mercy on me, a
  son/daughter.
Lord Jesus Christ, Son of God, have mercy on me, a saint.

The Question

Do you tend to be more and more at home with the way the world works in the present evil age—in other words, is it working for you? Or less and less at home with it?

Stop and Help the Homeless Guy

LUKE 16:13–31 | "No one can serve two masters. Either you will hate the one and love the other, or you will be devoted to the one and despise the other. You cannot serve both God and money."

The Pharisees, who loved money, heard all this and were sneering at Jesus. He said to them, "You are the ones who justify yourselves in the eyes of others, but God knows your hearts. What people value highly is detestable in God's sight.

"The Law and the Prophets were proclaimed until John. Since that time, the good news of the kingdom of God is being preached, and everyone is forcing their way into it. It is easier for heaven and earth to disappear than for the least stroke of a pen to drop out of the Law.

"Anyone who divorces his wife and marries another woman commits adultery, and the man who marries a divorced woman commits adultery.

"There was a rich man who was dressed in purple and fine linen and lived in luxury every day. At his gate was laid a beggar named Lazarus, covered with sores and longing to eat what fell from the rich man's table. Even the dogs came and licked his sores.

"The time came when the beggar died and the angels carried him to Abraham's side. The rich man also died and was buried. In Hades, where he was in torment, he looked up and saw Abraham far away, with Lazarus by his side. So he called to him, 'Father Abraham, have pity on me and send Lazarus to dip the tip of his finger in water and cool my tongue, because I am in agony in this fire.'

"But Abraham replied, 'Son, remember that in your lifetime you received your good things, while Lazarus received bad things, but now he is comforted here and you are in agony. And besides all this, between us and you a great chasm has been set in place, so that those who want to go from here to you cannot, nor can anyone cross over from there to us.'

"He answered, 'Then I beg you, father, send Lazarus to my family, for I have five brothers. Let him warn them, so that they will not also come to this place of torment.'

"Abraham replied, 'They have Moses and the Prophets; let them listen to them.'

"'No, father Abraham,' he said, 'but if someone from the dead goes to them, they will repent.'

"He said to him, 'If they do not listen to Moses and the Prophets, they will not be convinced even if someone rises from the dead.'"

Consider This

What was his name?

Every morning on my way to work and every afternoon on my way home I pass him by. He is a homeless man. He sells a weekly newspaper. The paper is written by homeless men and women. My neighbor down the street in my last neighborhood is the editor of the paper. To qualify to sell the papers you must be homeless (or at least you must have been when you started).

Each day as I approach the intersection I remind myself that I don't have any cash in my car. I avoid eye contact as much as possible and when the light changes I head for home. I know he's going to be there. You can set your clock by him. I know I only need a dollar to buy a paper. So why don't I take the time to pick up a few quarters from my bedside table, put them in my pocket, and buy a paper once a week; or even once in a while? I think about it every day and yet I still haven't managed to do it.

This parable strikes me with haunting similarities. How many times did the rich man pass by Lazarus, the homeless man, without so much as a nod? How many times did the rich man think to himself how easy it would be to do something, anything, to help him? He never managed to do it.

It's so easy for me to villainize this unnamed rich man, whose crime had nothing to do with being rich and everything to do with not caring. Strangely, it's so easy for me to excuse my upper middle class, minivan-driving self for passing by the homeless man selling dollar newspapers on my way to pick up a five-dollar grande five-pump, no-water chai latte with a shot of espresso before I head into the office.

I've got another chance tomorrow.

Lord Jesus Christ, Son of God, have mercy on me, a sinner.

P.S. His name was Lazarus. And the rich man's name? Nobody cares.

The Prayer

Lord Jesus Christ, Son of God, have mercy on me, a sinner.
Lord Jesus Christ, Son of God, have mercy on me, a
son/daughter.
Lord Jesus Christ, Son of God, have mercy on me, a saint.

The Question

Do you tend to see people in apparent need or not see them? Or do you see them and try to ignore and avoid them? What might that say about you?

Listen to the Coach

25

LUKE 17:1–10 | Jesus said to his disciples: "Things that cause people to stumble are bound to come, but woe to anyone through whom they come. It would be better for them to be thrown into the sea with a millstone tied around their neck than to cause one of these little ones to stumble. So watch yourselves.

"If your brother or sister sins against you, rebuke them; and if they repent, forgive them. Even if they sin against you seven times in a day and seven times come back to you saying 'I repent,' you must forgive them."

The apostles said to the Lord, "Increase our faith!"

He replied, "If you have faith as small as a mustard seed, you can say to this mulberry tree, 'Be uprooted and planted in the sea,' and it will obey you.

"Suppose one of you has a servant plowing or looking after the sheep. Will he say to the servant when he comes in from the field, 'Come along now and sit down to eat'? Won't he rather say, 'Prepare my supper, get yourself ready and wait on me while I eat and drink; after that you may eat and drink'? Will he thank the servant because he did what he was told to do? So you also, when you have done everything you were told to do, should say, 'We are unworthy servants; we have only done our duty.'"

Consider This

Any time any of our children participate in sports activities, I stress a single piece of counsel to them over and over and over. "Listen to the coach." "Keep your eye on the ball" runs a close second. Nothing is more important, though, than keenly listening to the coach.

These series of teachings have the feel of a coach instructing athletes. Jesus is always teaching, ever making disciples. He invites us to listen to him in the same way his first disciples did. While we do not get Jesus in the flesh, we do have the distinctive advantage of both hindsight and the Holy Spirit. Those disciples didn't know what was going to happen in Jerusalem and beyond. We do. Those disciples didn't have the indwelling presence of the Holy Spirit. We do. With the written Word and through the presence of the Spirit, Jesus operates as a master coach.

Let's break down the four basic lessons he's teaching us today:

1. When it comes to "these little ones," the poor and blind and crippled and destitute, we must always come to their

aid and never oppose them. All the brokenness of the world works against them constantly. They need mercy rather than pity, friends and not additional foes.

2. Do not separate yourself from sinners. Sinners do not make you unclean, rather your refusal to forgive them makes you unusable in service to God's kingdom. The well of God's mercy never runs dry even for those who most oppose him. It takes divine capacity to forgive like God forgives. Never stop forgiving.

3. Faith is a way of living in anticipation of the ever-unfolding work of God. Faith is not a passive belief system to which one gives their intellectual assent. Faith is actively doing #1, #2, and #4.

4. Don't expect to be applauded and celebrated for merely doing your job. Affirmation may come. Receive it when it does, but do not expect it. We serve. It's what we do. We renounce any sense of entitlement, and we reject the ever-present temptation to seek status and honor from well doing.

While it's not complicated, it's not easy either. This is discipleship in good form. These ways of life go against the grain of the patterns of the world.

And by the way, in case you missed it, the opposite of all four of these life ethics can be summed up in one word: Pharisees.

Be on your guard. Watch yourselves. Listen, the coach beckons us. The yeast of the Pharisees is always right there, and it doesn't take much to leaven the whole loaf.

The Prayer
Lord Jesus Christ, Son of God, have mercy on me, a sinner.
Lord Jesus Christ, Son of God, have mercy on me, a
  son/daughter.
Lord Jesus Christ, Son of God, have mercy on me, a saint.

The Question
Which one of these four basic lessons from today speaks most to you in your life right now? Why? How might you respond?

26 Act as If

LUKE 17:11–19 | Now on his way to Jerusalem, Jesus traveled along the border between Samaria and Galilee. As he was going into a village, ten men who had leprosy met him. They stood at a distance and called out in a loud voice, "Jesus, Master, have pity on us!"

When he saw them, he said, "Go, show yourselves to the priests." And as they went, they were cleansed.

One of them, when he saw he was healed, came back, praising God in a loud voice. He threw himself at Jesus' feet and thanked him—and he was a Samaritan.

Jesus asked, "Were not all ten cleansed? Where are the other nine? Has no one returned to give praise to God except this foreigner?" Then he said to him, "Rise and go; your faith has made you well."

Consider This

We are about to enter the home stretch and make the turn into Jerusalem. It's been a long and meandering journey for Jesus and his disciples. They have traversed between the impeccably religious and the ignominious rejects. They've been entertained in the homes of the social elite, and they've walked among the tombs to cast out legions of satanic demons. In one breath Jesus rebukes the proud, and in the next he restores the poor.

This journey sounds familiar, doesn't it? It's the same world we live in. We walk down those same paths—the in-group and the outcasts, the incomprehensibly wealthy and the inconsolably broken. We, too, want to associate with people who raise our social profile, and there are more than a few kinds of people we don't want to be caught dead with.

Through it all, from there to here and from then to now, we have labored to keep our focus on the one necessary thing: listening to Jesus, the Son of God, the Messiah. From the first century to the twenty-first, following Jesus is truly an extraordinary thing.

In today's text he teaches us another profound lesson. You will remember yesterday his disciples asked him to increase their faith. He responded by telling them they needed but a tiny mustard seed's worth to move heaven and earth. It's another way of saying faith is not an asset we build and hold on to. Faith is not mere belief, but human activity born of confidence in God's possibilities.

Tomorrow he will draw from the drama of a court of law to teach us yet another lesson about faith. Today, however, we get a glimpse of exactly what the kind of faith he is looking for looks like. Here are the words I want us to listen carefully to: *"Go show yourselves to the priests."*

You read the text. Listen to the lepers' cry of faith: *"Jesus, Master, have pity on us!"* It sounds like the prayer we've been praying every day. The most theologically astute minds in the country missed what these untouchable exiles got. They knew his name. They knew his rank. And they knew their need. *"Jesus, Master, have pity on us!"* Despite all their misfortune and countless losses, they had not given up on the tender mercy of a compassionate God.

All Jesus had to do was say the word. Their predetermined posture had formed itself into a kind of preemptive obedience.

"Go show yourselves to the priests."

This is the remarkable part. He told them to do what a leper who was cleansed would do—to go to the temple and have a priest certify their cure and readmit them into the community. They didn't close their eyes for a time of prayer and meditation. They didn't look down and gaze at their skin to see if the miracle was actually happening. They simply went. They didn't need a sign or proof or even reassurance to just do it. They just did it. The next seven words tell the story: *And as they went, they were cleansed.*

They didn't wait for God to do something before they acted. They acted in anticipation of God doing something. We so often find ourselves in a posture of saying, "God, if you will do this, I will do that." A slight and equally errant variation on the prayer says, "I will do this if you will do that." All the while, God is saying, "I'll do that when you do this."

We're asking Jesus to write a check while he's telling us the check has been written. All that remains to do is to cash it. People tend to get it exactly backward, thinking if we can name it, God will claim it for us. The name-it-and-claim-it approach only works when God does the naming. Faith is the actual activity of doing the claiming.

The will of God can only be known by listening to the Word of God. Until we do that, our prayers are at best, wishes. Until our lives find their deepest moorings in the Word of God and our greatest delight in doing the will of God, our best-laid intentions to have faith result in little more than empty, easy "believism."

These ten lepers acted "as-if." They moved as though the miracle had happened. And it only happened as they moved. *And as they went, they were cleansed.* If they had waited for their cure to come first, they would still be standing there.

There's so much more to learn from Jesus in this story and, by the mercy of God, Jesus will bring us back to this place again. The only necessary thing now is to act on what we have learned. The interesting thing about the Hebrew word for "obey" is it means "to hear."

So where in your life might Jesus be calling you to act as-if? Are you listening? It's the most important thing in your life right now.

Lord Jesus Christ, Son of God, have mercy on me, a sinner.

The Prayer

Lord Jesus Christ, Son of God, have mercy on me, a sinner.
Lord Jesus Christ, Son of God, have mercy on me, a son/daughter.
Lord Jesus Christ, Son of God, have mercy on me, a saint.

The Question

What effect or impact is our daily praying these prayers having on you? What about this notion of a predetermined posture of humility becoming a kind of preemptive obedience of faith?

27 It's Always Now or Never

LUKE 17:20–37 | Once, on being asked by the Pharisees when the kingdom of God would come, Jesus replied, "The coming of the kingdom of God is not something that can be observed, nor will people say, 'Here it is,' or 'There it is,' because the kingdom of God is in your midst."

Then he said to his disciples, "The time is coming when you will long to see one of the days of the Son of Man, but you will not see it. People will tell you, 'There he is!' or 'Here he is!' Do not go running off after them. For the Son of Man in his day will be like the lightning, which flashes and lights up the sky from one end to the other. But first he must suffer many things and be rejected by this generation.

"Just as it was in the days of Noah, so also will it be in the days of the Son of Man. People were eating, drinking, marrying and being given in marriage up to the day Noah entered the ark. Then the flood came and destroyed them all.

"It was the same in the days of Lot. People were eating and drinking, buying and selling, planting and building. But the day Lot left Sodom, fire and sulfur rained down from heaven and destroyed them all.

"It will be just like this on the day the Son of Man is revealed. On that day no one who is on the housetop, with possessions inside, should go down to get them. Likewise, no one in the field should go back for anything. Remember Lot's wife! Whoever tries to keep their life will lose it, and whoever loses their life will preserve it. I tell you, on that night two people will be in one bed; one will be taken and the other left. Two women will be grinding grain together; one will be taken and the other left."

"Where, Lord?" they asked.

He replied, "Where there is a dead body, there the vultures will gather."

Consider This

The kingdom of God will be in us now or it may never be in us at all.

For my money, this pretty much sums up what I'm hearing from Jesus in today's text.

In their quest for control, the Pharisees want signs. They want to get it in their date books. To this question, Jesus says two things. First, the kingdom of God is not an event somewhere in the future. Second, the kingdom of God is now, at hand, present, and in your midst. We get Jesus' first sermon, a total of seventeen words, from Mark's gospel. Here it is: "The time has come," he said. "The kingdom of God has come near. Repent and believe the good news!" (Mark 1:15).

This is what this journey to Jerusalem has been all about. Jesus is making disciples of the kingdom of God. He is training men and women to live under the gracious rule of God. He is preparing us for eternal life in the kingdom, which is already here and still yet to come in all its glory.

He's effectively saying: the kingdom of God will be in us now or it may never be in us at all.

Repentance means turning away from the broken world order, from the corruption of the present evil age, and aligning one's life with the now present kingdom of God. When the kingdom finally comes in all its glorious fullness, it will be too late to decide.

In a very real sense, Jesus is ever saying, "It's now or never." Why do I say this? Because of the stories Jesus cites.

"Just as it was in the days of Noah, so also will it be in the days of the Son of Man. People were eating, drinking, marrying and being given in marriage up to the day Noah entered the ark. Then the flood came and destroyed them all.

"It was the same in the days of Lot. People were eating and drinking, buying and selling, planting and building. But the day Lot left Sodom, fire and sulfur rained down from heaven and destroyed them all."

See what I mean? It's always now or never. Why? Two reasons: Noah and Lot. Everything was rolling along just like always until it wasn't. In what seems like an instant, everything changed. Eating, drinking, buying, selling, marrying, planting, and building are all good things. That's what we do. It's ordinary, everyday, garden variety life. Then it will happen, the Son of Man will come, like a thief in the night. Is this because Jesus wants to catch people off guard? Heavens no! He's telling us all of this in order to prevent that from happening.

It's always now or never. There's an urgency. Follow Jesus now.

All of this reminds me of my favorite C. S. Lewis quote. I'll end with it.

When the author walks on to the stage the play is over. God is going to invade, all right: but what is the good of saying you are on His side then, when you see the whole natural universe melting away like a dream and something else—something it never entered your head to conceive—comes crashing in; something so beautiful to some of us and so terrible to others that none of us will have any choice left? For this time it will be God without disguise; something so overwhelming that it will strike either irresistible love or irresistible horror into every creature. It will be too late then to choose your side. There is no use saying you choose to lie down when it has become impossible to stand up. That will not be the time for choosing; it will be the time when we discover which side we really have chosen, whether we realised it before or not. Now, today, this moment, is our chance to choose the right side. God is holding back to give us that chance. It will not last forever. We must take it or leave it. (*Mere Christianity* [Harper Collins, 2001], 65)

It's always now or never.

The Prayer

Lord Jesus Christ, Son of God, have mercy on me, a sinner.
Lord Jesus Christ, Son of God, have mercy on me, a son/daughter.
Lord Jesus Christ, Son of God, have mercy on me, a saint.

The Question

What do you make of this now or never quality of the kingdom of God? How does this affect your sense of urgency?

Measure Down

LUKE 18:1–17 | Then Jesus told his disciples a parable to show them that they should always pray and not give up. He said: "In a certain town there was a judge who neither feared God nor cared what people thought. And there was a widow in that town who kept coming to him with the plea, 'Grant me justice against my adversary.'

"For some time he refused. But finally he said to himself, 'Even though I don't fear God or care what people think, yet because this widow keeps bothering me, I will see that she gets justice, so that she won't eventually come and attack me!'"

And the Lord said, "Listen to what the unjust judge says. And will not God bring about justice for his chosen ones, who cry out to him day and night? Will he keep putting them off? I tell you, he will see that they get justice, and quickly. However, when the Son of Man comes, will he find faith on the earth?"

To some who were confident of their own righteousness and looked down on everyone else, Jesus told this parable: "Two men went up to the temple to pray, one a Pharisee and the other a tax collector. The Pharisee stood by himself and prayed: 'God, I thank you that I am not like other people—robbers, evil-doers, adulterers—or even like this tax collector. I fast twice a week and give a tenth of all I get.'

"But the tax collector stood at a distance. He would not even look up to heaven, but beat his breast and said, 'God, have mercy on me, a sinner.'

"I tell you that this man, rather than the other, went home justified before God. For all those who exalt themselves will be humbled, and those who humble themselves will be exalted."

People were also bringing babies to Jesus for him to place his hands on them. When the disciples saw this, they rebuked them. But Jesus called the children to him and said, "Let the little children come to me, and do not hinder them, for the kingdom of God belongs to such as these. Truly I tell you, anyone who will not receive the kingdom of God like a little child will never enter it."

Consider This

We live in a world where all the energy goes into measuring up. Who has the most credentials, the best résumé, the highest grades, the top salary, and on we could go.

Meanwhile, Jesus establishes a kingdom where all the energy goes into measuring down.

The world works like a kid at an amusement park standing in a roller coaster line just hoping and praying that they will measure up to the height line to be admitted to the ride.

It reminds me of a story I once heard about the Pulitzer–Prize-winning author David McCullough. He does all his writing in a small primitive cabin that sits behind his residence at the end of a trail. As the trail ends, one comes to a gate and next to the gate is a measuring rod with a sign. The sign says you must be no taller than the mark in order to be admitted. In other words, you must measure down. (Only his grandchildren can get in.)

If there's one consistent message in all Jesus has said thus far in this journey from Transfiguration Mountain to the Mount of Golgotha, it is this: measure down. In today's text he puts it this way: *"Truly I tell you, anyone who will not receive the kingdom of God like a little child will never enter it."*

As I've said before, he's not talking about becoming carefree and whimsical and full of childlike wonder, though that's a good thing. No, Jesus is saying the only way you can get into his kingdom is to come in the same way a child does— with no qualifications save the one qualification of having no qualifications to commend you. In the first century, children had no status or rights or regard from the society. The Pharisees, as well as Jesus' disciples, routinely handled them like a bouncer would, pushing them out of the way.

Jesus will not have it. Along the journey, Jesus has pointed out example after example of what he's looking for and who he's not. The kingdom exemplars he identifies are women, widows, beggars, lepers, tax collectors, prostitutes, crippled, children, demon-possessed and oppressed, and so on. Today's text is filled with it. Today it's a powerless albeit persistent widow and a despicable, shame-filled tax collector. Contrast that with an unrighteous, dishonest, powerful judge and a meticulously careful and proud rule-follower Pharisee.

I don't know about you, but I have given much of my life to the quest of measuring up. I think I'm really only on the cusp of learning what it means to measure down. "But you are a teacher of the Word of God," you say. And I say, "Yes, so were the scribes and Pharisees." My ability (or not) to teach Scripture and minister the Word of God no more qualifies me to enter God's kingdom than a rich person's wealth or an important person's status or a do-gooder's do-gooding qualifies them.

Jesus is not telling us we have to become status-less or poor or widowed or afflicted with leprosy or a child in order to enter his kingdom. He's saying we must become like them in this respect: we claim no right to anything and depend on God's mercy for everything. To the extent we cannot become detached from all of our wealth and status and otherwise highly valued qualifications, we must divorce ourselves from them. (We will see that one in play tomorrow.)

When we finally learn to value ourselves only in the way we are valued by God and not by all the metrics the world uses to deem some worthy and others worthless, we will have finally measured down. When we finally understand we are the same as all the people that our distinctions have distinguished us from, we will finally have learned that they measure up. When we finally learn to value the least among us in the same way we value ourselves, then we will have entered the kingdom of God.

And in the end, this will be the only kingdom still standing. Trust me when I say, we will want to be in that number. We must learn to sing the song now.

The Prayer

Lord Jesus Christ, Son of God, have mercy on me, a sinner.
Lord Jesus Christ, Son of God, have mercy on me, a
    son/daughter.
Lord Jesus Christ, Son of God, have mercy on me, a saint.

The Question

Reflect on this claim: When we finally learn to value ourselves only in the way we are valued by God and not by all the metrics the world uses to deem some worthy and others worthless, we will have finally measured down.

Fifth Sunday of Lent

Let People Go Away Sad

LUKE 18:18–30 | A certain ruler asked him, "Good teacher, what must I do to inherit eternal life?"

"Why do you call me good?" Jesus answered. "No one is good—except God alone. You know the commandments: 'You shall not commit adultery, you shall not murder, you shall not steal, you shall not give false testimony, honor your father and mother.'"

"All these I have kept since I was a boy," he said.

When Jesus heard this, he said to him, "You still lack one thing. Sell everything you have and give to the poor, and you will have treasure in heaven. Then come, follow me."

When he heard this, he became very sad, because he was very wealthy. Jesus looked at him and said, "How hard it is for the rich to enter the kingdom of God! Indeed, it is easier for a camel to go through the eye of a needle than for someone who is rich to enter the kingdom of God."

Those who heard this asked, "Who then can be saved?"

Jesus replied, "What is impossible with man is possible with God."

Peter said to him, "We have left all we had to follow you!"

"Truly I tell you," Jesus said to them, "no one who has left home or wife or brothers or sisters or parents or children for the sake of the kingdom of God will fail to receive many times as much in this age, and in the age to come eternal life."

Consider This

I've thought about this a lot in recent years. Let's say I was leading a church and this same rich young ruler came forward after a service and asked me, "What must I do to inherit eternal life?" How would I answer that question?

For that matter, what if this same person came forward at an evangelistic crusade and asked the same question? What answer would they get?

In both cases, the person would likely be led in a prayer that goes something like the following:

> Dear Lord Jesus, I know that I am a sinner, and I ask for your forgiveness. I believe you died for my sins and rose from the dead. I turn from my sins and invite you to come into my heart and life. I want to trust and follow you as my Lord and Savior. In your name. Amen.

We would give them some literature and encourage them to become active in the local church, and that would be that. Okay, we might try and interest them in a large gift to the building campaign! This has been the basic shape of evangelism and discipleship in the North American evangelical church for the past fifty years.

Notice how drastically different Jesus answers the question: *"You still lack one thing. Sell everything you have and give to the poor, and you will have treasure in heaven. Then come, follow me."*

How do we reconcile such a disparity between what Jesus says and the conventional practice of today? I don't think we can.

Doesn't it strike you as a bit dangerous to depart so drastically from Jesus' approach? All things equal, wouldn't we be giving the rich ruler a profoundly false sense of security in their eternal salvation? At the same time, I can't picture myself responding in the same way Jesus did.

So what if this entire sinner's prayer approach to eternal salvation is all wrong? I mean, it's not actually in the Bible anywhere, nor do we see it anywhere in the early church or church history for that matter.

On the other hand, surely salvation can't come down to money and one's relative attachment or detachment from it. Justification by grace through faith would go right out the window if selling everything one had and giving it to the poor were a requirement. So what gives here?

My take: I don't think salvation is such a transactional reality. I think it's far more relational. Can a person come to faith in an instant? Sure. Love at first sight happens. More often than not, though, I think it takes time. Maybe it takes following Jesus for more than a church service or two to be ready to offer up your entire allegiance to him. What if a little bit of discipleship (i.e., following Jesus) actually opens up the door for evangelism to happen rather than the reverse case?

Let me suggest a few assumptions that might change our take on the passage at hand. First, I think it's fair to assume that the rich ruler was following Jesus. He was in the midst of the people that day and had the courage to bring forth his question. Chances are, he had been there before. Second, we know he went away sad, but we don't know how it actually turned out in the end. Maybe he came back around. Maybe he realized his wealth actually had him and that Jesus was right and he had to do something drastic to escape its gravity. Maybe he came to grips with the hard reality that his money stood between himself and Jesus.

That's how I'm thinking about it. What if we didn't feel like we had to soft-pedal Jesus when he says unreasonable things like this? What if we just let Jesus be Jesus? What if we just listened to him instead of explaining how he couldn't possibly mean what he said? What if we were willing to let people go away sad when something Jesus says makes them sad? What if we could let them sit in that sadness a bit? What if we could sit with them in that sadness a bit? What if that's actually what real discipleship is all about—feeling the weight of the cross a bit, counting the cost, weighing allegiances, making hard yet life-giving choices?

I'm obviously still thinking this through. And the more I think about it, the more I am led back to our Jesus prayers.

The Prayer

Lord Jesus Christ, Son of God, have mercy on me, a sinner.
Lord Jesus Christ, Son of God, have mercy on me, a
son/daughter.
Lord Jesus Christ, Son of God, have mercy on me, a saint.

The Question

Where in your life right now do you need to feel the gravity of Jesus' teaching and the weight of the cross? Where is his teaching hitting you hardest?

We've Never Been Here Before

29

LUKE 18:31–33 | Jesus took the Twelve aside and told them, "We are going up to Jerusalem, and everything that is written by the prophets about the Son of Man will be fulfilled. He will be delivered over to the Gentiles. They will mock him, insult him and spit on him; they will flog him and kill him. On the third day he will rise again."

The disciples did not understand any of this. Its meaning was hidden from them, and they did not know what he was talking about.

Consider This

It's like déjà vu.

> "Let these words sink into your ears: The Son of Man is going to be delivered into the hands of men." But they did not understand this saying, and it was concealed from them, so that they might not perceive it. And they were afraid to ask him about this saying. (Luke 9:44–45 ESV)

That happened weeks back just following the ascent to Transfiguration Mountain when we began this journey to the cross.

You may have noticed over the course of these weeks that Jesus makes disciples in plain view of the public. He's not sequestered off in some synagogue somewhere waxing eloquent before a captive audience. He's teaching his disciples in the presence of the religious establishment. At times he will turn and address the Pharisees. At other times he speaks directly to a leper or a prostitute or a crippled person or, like yesterday, a rich ruler. Typically, though, it's all happening at the same time in the same settings.

Very rarely does Jesus pull his disciples aside and address them privately. It is significant that he does so in both of these instances above and tells them the same thing. Even more significant is the way the disciples' response has not changed at all despite all that has happened.

Despite the fact he made it crystal clear, the reality that Jesus is going to die is the furthest thing from their mind. It's so easy with all these years of hindsight to think it's an open-and-shut case when it comes to our own understanding—to think we get it.

I think what I want to suggest is that getting it is a never-ending process. Yes, we get it at some level. Speaking for myself only, I am increasingly sure that what I do get pales in comparison to what I don't yet grasp.

This is the great mystery of our faith: Christ has died! Christ is risen! Christ will come again!

Come on. A God who dies? God and mortality just don't mix. A God who humbles himself? God and humility just don't mix. A God who becomes a human being? Those categories are mutually exclusive. So many of us have been around this story for so long it's challenging to still see it freshly. I am beginning to think a mark of maturity in following Jesus is this: The further we follow him, the more we grasp the mystery; yet the more we grasp the mystery, the more we realize the vastness of what we can't comprehend.

So what if genuine growth and true maturity not only begins but continues with the confession that no matter how much we do grasp, there's far more that we don't?

We haven't been here. We haven't done this. And we don't have the T-shirt. As we near Jerusalem and all that will unfold there, let's begin praying for grace to hear with new ears and see with fresh eyes and behold with deeper humility this great mystery like never before. We've done Easter before, but not this Easter. Stay with it now, more than ever:

The Prayer
Lord Jesus Christ, Son of God, have mercy on me, a sinner.

137

*Lord Jesus Christ, Son of God, have mercy on me, a
  son/daughter.*
Lord Jesus Christ, Son of God, have mercy on me, a saint.

The Question

How about you? Do you really see that there's far more to
get than you've got when it comes to following Jesus, or is
it just easy to agree with the sentiment? Are you following
harder after him now or still just sort of?

30 Answer His Question

LUKE 18:35–43 | As Jesus approached Jericho, a blind man
was sitting by the roadside begging. When he heard the crowd
going by, he asked what was happening. They told him, "Jesus
of Nazareth is passing by."

He called out, "Jesus, Son of David, have mercy on me!"

Those who led the way rebuked him and told him to be quiet,
but he shouted all the more, "Son of David, have mercy on me!"

Jesus stopped and ordered the man to be brought to him. When
he came near, Jesus asked him, "What do you want me to do
for you?"

"Lord, I want to see," he replied.

Jesus said to him, "Receive your sight; your faith has healed you."

Immediately he received his sight and followed Jesus, praising God. When all the people saw it, they also praised God.

Consider This

The last miracle before Jerusalem. Finally, with the healing of a blind man, Jesus completes the fulfillment of the prophecy of Isaiah we began with back in Luke 4. We will spend a day in Jericho, visit the home of the "wee little man" Zacchaeus, and then on to the city that kills the prophets and stones those sent to her.

Imagine how surprised I was at this point near the end of the journey to see our daily prayer through these days come off the lips of a blind beggar.

"Jesus, Son of David, have mercy on me!"

Wow! You will have to believe me when I tell you this was completely unplanned. I do believe it has been orchestrated by the Holy Spirit.

The crowd couldn't have cared less for this man. In fact, they tried to shut him down, treating him as a nuisance. He shouts louder.

"Son of David, have mercy on me!"

Jesus stops everything and orders the man be brought to him. Then and now, the Suffering One always makes a beeline to the suffering ones. Then and now, the privileged ones turn a blind eye to them. When will we learn? The kingdom of God, inaugurated by the Son of God, literally turns everything around.

Over the course of the four Gospels, we find somewhere around one hundred questions Jesus asks people. Of all of them, this one in today's text is my favorite: *When he came near, Jesus asked him, "What do you want me to do for you?"*

It has never occurred to me to ask a person in need this question. I usually assume I know what they need, do that (or not), and move on. What if the next time I encounter a person in need I stop, take the time to see them, and ask this question, "What do you want me to do for you?" The question is as alarming as it is disarming.

I think I'm going to start asking that question of others all the time, because the truth is we are all in need of everyday expressions of mercy and grace. Mercy, however, cannot be equated with what I think they need. Mercy must be defined by them. In many ways this question gives them the gift of speaking the particularity of their need. I honestly can't remember the last time someone asked me this specific question. Can you?

Jesus is ever and always asking this question. "What do you want me to do for you?" He asks it to others through us. And he asks it of us through others. But today, he asks it directly to you.

"What do you want me to do for you?"

How do you respond? Sit with that question.

I love the pointed simplicity of the blind man's answer. *"Lord, I want to see."*

That's a good response for us as we make the turn to Jerusalem. Lord, I want to see.

The Prayer

Lord Jesus Christ, Son of God, have mercy on me, a sinner.
Lord Jesus Christ, Son of God, have mercy on me, a
    son/daughter.
Lord Jesus Christ, Son of God, have mercy on me, a saint.

The Question

So Jesus wants to know: What do you want him to do for you? Be specific.

Be Careful How You Read

31

LUKE 19:1–10 | Jesus entered Jericho and was passing through. A man was there by the name of Zacchaeus; he was a chief tax collector and was wealthy. He wanted to see who Jesus was, but because he was short he could not see over the crowd. So he ran ahead and climbed a sycamore-fig tree to see him, since Jesus was coming that way.

When Jesus reached the spot, he looked up and said to him, "Zacchaeus, come down immediately. I must stay at your house today." So he came down at once and welcomed him gladly.

All the people saw this and began to mutter, "He has gone to be the guest of a sinner."

But Zacchaeus stood up and said to the Lord, "Look, Lord! Here and now I give half of my possessions to the poor, and if I have cheated anybody out of anything, I will pay back four times the amount."

Jesus said to him, "Today salvation has come to this house, because this man, too, is a son of Abraham. For the Son of Man came to seek and to save the lost."

Consider This

Zacchaeus gets a bad rap. I think it's undeserved.

I cannot overemphasize the importance of reading the Bible carefully. Once we see things in a certain way, it is hard to un-see them that way again. I don't know about you, but for most of my Bible-reading life I've seen Zacchaeus as a "wee little man" who was a lying, cheating, stealing, low-down dirty scoundrel of a tax collector. And did I mention stealing? Everybody hated him.

Why have I thought this? Well, for starters, he as much as admitted it, didn't he, when he said he would give half of his possessions to the poor and pay back anyone he had cheated four times the amount. Wasn't that pretty much an admission of guilt? After all, wasn't that why Jesus went to his house—to scold him into changing his ways?

As I learn from my own teachers to read more carefully, I am beginning to see Zach a bit differently. Most translations of Luke 19:8 translate the Greek verb for "give" as the present tense verb that it is. In other words, instead of Zacchaeus saying, "I will give half of my possessions to the poor," he actually said, "I give half of my possessions to the poor." The same can be said of the latter report where he actually says, "I pay back four times the amount to anybody I have cheated."

Zacchaeus is telling Jesus of his present policy and practice as relates to money. Here's a wealthy person who gives away half of his possessions to the poor. He tithes 50 percent to the needy. Meanwhile, everybody around has him in the category of sinner, which effectively means scumbag outcast. Nowhere is there a report that Zach actually cheated anyone. Whether or not he had done so before, this policy of paying back four times the amount seems more than fair. Given the kind of report he is offering here, he seems like the kind of guy who would catch and report his own errors. Think about it. Why would a guy who gives half of his holdings to the poor turn around and cheat them on their taxes?

When Jesus called out his name and said he wanted to come over, that was all good news to Zacchaeus. He "welcomed him gladly," we are told. One would think if Zacchaeus was the scuzzball everyone said, he would have been mortified that Jesus wanted to come to his house.

So rather than this being a repentance to salvation story as it is commonly read, it now looks like a vindication to restoration to salvation story. The only people who seem in need of repentance are the grumblers who are angry that Jesus went to see him. When Jesus recognizes Zacchaeus as a "son of Abraham," he basically restores him to the community.

In short, just like with the widows and the prostitutes and the Samaritan leper and the tax collector in the temple and the blind beggar, Jesus adds Zacchaeus to the list of all-stars you want to be like. It's worth pointing out that Zacchaeus, unlike the rich ruler of a few days back, is an example of a wealthy person who hits the mark. And the grumbling crowd? They get added to the naughty list.

The long and short of today's lesson: be careful how you read because it will determine how you lead.

It turns out Zacchaeus wasn't such a wee little man after all. At least he's got a pretty big heart.

The Prayer

Lord Jesus Christ, Son of God, have mercy on me, a sinner.
Lord Jesus Christ, Son of God, have mercy on me, a
*   son/daughter.*
Lord Jesus Christ, Son of God, have mercy on me, a saint.

The Question

So what do you think of Zacchaeus now? How does this impact your approach of reading Scripture more carefully?

32 Become a Holy Risk-Taker

LUKE 19:11–27 ESV | As they heard these things, he proceeded to tell a parable, because he was near to Jerusalem, and because they supposed that the kingdom of God was to appear immediately. He said therefore, "A nobleman went into a far country to receive for himself a kingdom and then return. Calling ten of his servants, he gave them ten minas, and said to them, 'Engage in business until I come.' But his citizens hated him and sent a delegation after him, saying, 'We do not want this man to reign over us.' When he returned, having received the kingdom, he ordered these servants to whom he had given the money to be called to him, that he might know what they had gained by doing business. The first came before him, saying, 'Lord, your mina has made ten minas more.' And he said to him, 'Well done, good servant! Because you have been faithful in a very little, you shall have authority over ten cities.' And the second came, saying, 'Lord, your mina has made five minas.' And he said to him, 'And you are to be over five cities.' Then another came, saying, 'Lord, here is your mina, which I kept laid away in a handkerchief; for I was afraid of you, because you are a severe man. You take what you did not deposit, and reap what you did not sow.' He said to him, 'I will condemn you with your own words, you wicked servant! You knew that I was a severe man, taking what I did not deposit and reaping what I did not sow? Why then did you not put my money in the bank, and at my coming I might have collected it with interest?' And he said to those who stood by, 'Take the mina from him, and give it to the one who has the ten minas.' And they said to him, 'Lord, he has ten minas!' 'I tell you that to everyone who has, more will be given, but from the one who has not, even what he has will be taken away. But as for these enemies of mine, who did not want me to reign over them, bring them here and slaughter them before me.'"

Consider This

In the kingdom of God, the greatest risk is taking no risk at all.

The parable in today's text is pretty straightforward. Permit me a loosely correlated analogy putting it in today's terms. A mina would come to about four months' wages for one of these servants. For purposes of this analogy, a mina equals whatever you make in four months.

Let's say I make $10,000 a month. That makes my mina worth $40,000. Now suppose my boss gave me an additional $40,000 and instructed me to use this money to make more for the company. In other words, it was not my money but the company's. My job was to take the company's money and make the company more money. So far so good.

What do I do? Should I buy a car wash? How about a herd of cattle? Maybe I should consider a multi-level marketing pyramid scheme with some new health revolutionizing drink? Or I could just put it into securities like Facebook or Tesla or Apple. Then again, I could just buy a whole lot of Powerball lottery tickets. What will I do? Where is the most intelligent, promising risk?

How about you? It doesn't seem like giving the money away is an option here. Do you make a safe play or take a big risk? There's only one wrong response in this scenario: doing nothing with the money.

What if I came to the realization that the money I thought was mine was not mine after all? What if I finally realized it all belonged to God yet had been entrusted to me? And what if I understood God wanted me to use God's money to do things that produced a return for his kingdom? How would that change the way I handled money?

I know a man of extraordinary wealth who uses his exceptional investment skills to make more money all for the purposes of investing it into promising ventures serving the kingdom of God. It's extraordinary to behold, and he keeps making more and more money. The more he makes, the more he gives. There's no percentage limit like a tithe. I sometimes wonder if he even keeps a tithe for himself.

It makes me wonder what it would be like if I even invested a tithe, 10 percent, of the money entrusted to me for the sake of God's kingdom—not giving it, mind you, but risking it or trading on it? It sounds fun, but if I'm honest I've got to admit this has never occurred to me before. I live with a binary mentality as it comes to money. I either keep it for my own uses or I give it away. What if there were a category between for-profit and non-profit? What if I had a genuine for-faith mentality, risking resources for the sake of a greater return to the kingdom of God?

I know this may not be exactly what the parable in today's text is talking about. On the other hand, maybe it is. Jesus is teaching us disciples what it means to be a holy risk-taker for the sake of his kingdom in the period between his first coming and second coming. It can be about money, but it can also be about the kinds of gifts, talents, and abilities God has given us.

One thing is for sure. The only risk we never want to take is the risk of not risking at all.

The Prayer

Lord Jesus Christ, Son of God, have mercy on me, a sinner.
Lord Jesus Christ, Son of God, have mercy on me, a
*   son/daughter.*
Lord Jesus Christ, Son of God, have mercy on me, a saint.

The Question

How might you become more of a risk-taker when it comes to sowing for a great awakening to the kingdom of God?

33 Get Ready for the Great Reversal

LUKE 19:28–44 | After Jesus had said this, he went on ahead, going up to Jerusalem. As he approached Bethphage and Bethany at the hill called the Mount of Olives, he sent two of his disciples, saying to them, "Go to the village ahead of you, and as you enter it, you will find a colt tied there, which no one has ever ridden. Untie it and bring it here. If anyone asks you, 'Why are you untying it?' say, 'The Lord needs it.'"

Those who were sent ahead went and found it just as he had told them. As they were untying the colt, its owners asked them, "Why are you untying the colt?"

They replied, "The Lord needs it."

They brought it to Jesus, threw their cloaks on the colt and put Jesus on it. As he went along, people spread their cloaks on the road.

When he came near the place where the road goes down the Mount of Olives, the whole crowd of disciples began joyfully to praise God in loud voices for all the miracles they had seen:

"Blessed is the king who comes in the name of the Lord!"

"Peace in heaven and glory in the highest!"

Some of the Pharisees in the crowd said to Jesus, "Teacher, rebuke your disciples!"

"I tell you," he replied, "if they keep quiet, the stones will cry out."

As he approached Jerusalem and saw the city, he wept over it and said, "If you, even you, had only known on this day what would bring you peace—but now it is hidden from your eyes. The days will come upon you when your enemies will build an embankment against you and encircle you and hem you in on every side. They will dash you to the ground, you and the children within your walls. They will not leave one stone on another, because you did not recognize the time of God's coming to you."

Consider This

I was glad when they said to me,
"Let us go to the house of the Lord!"

> Our feet have been standing
>> within your gates, O Jerusalem. (Ps. 122:1–2 ESV)

So many divine coincidences swirl in the air now. Jesus turns everything around.

As the gospel began, the Son of God rode on the back of a donkey in the womb of his mother. Today he rides into Jerusalem on the back of a colt.

In the beginning, the wise kings from foreign lands came to see the child born King of the Jews. Today he rides into Jerusalem hailed by the people, *"Blessed is the king who comes in the name of the Lord."*

In the beginning, the heavenly host of angelic beings shouted, "Glory to God in the highest heaven, and on earth, peace to those on whom his favor rests" (Luke 2:14). Today, the crowds of disciples declare, *"Peace in heaven and glory in the highest!"*

Jesus turns everything around. In the beginning he claimed the prophecy of Isaiah, "good news to the poor. He has sent me to proclaim freedom for the prisoners and recovery of sight for the blind, to set the oppressed free" (Luke 4:18). Today he enters the city of kings as the King of kings having fulfilled all of the prophecy and then some.

In the beginning, Simeon prophesied about him, "This child is destined to cause the falling and rising of many in Israel, and to be a sign that will be spoken against, so that the thoughts of many hearts will be revealed. And a sword will pierce your own soul too" (Luke 2:34–35). Today we stand on the eve of its fulfillment.

We have arrived at our destination; the journey is now complete. We will now behold him undertake that for which he came. The echoes of Isaiah via John the Baptist still resound in the sky,

"The voice of one calling in the wilderness,
'Prepare the way for the Lord,
    make his paths straight.
Every valley shall be filled,
    and every mountain and hill shall be made low,
and the crooked shall become straight,
    and the rough places shall become level ways,
and all flesh shall see the salvation of God.'"
    (Luke 3:4–6 ESV)

Get ready for the great reversal. Jesus turns everything around.

The Prayer

Lord Jesus Christ, Son of God, have mercy on me, a sinner.
Lord Jesus Christ, Son of God, have mercy on me, a
    son/daughter.
Lord Jesus Christ, Son of God, have mercy on me, a saint.

The Question

Time to ask again—are you still praying these prayers, or are they beginning to pray you? Reflect on how they are impacting you.

34 Invite Jesus to Church and Prepare Yourself

LUKE 19:45–20:18 | When Jesus entered the temple courts, he began to drive out those who were selling. "It is written," he said to them, "'My house will be a house of prayer'; but you have made it 'a den of robbers.'"

Every day he was teaching at the temple. But the chief priests, the teachers of the law and the leaders among the people were trying to kill him. Yet they could not find any way to do it, because all the people hung on his words.

One day as Jesus was teaching the people in the temple courts and proclaiming the good news, the chief priests and the teachers of the law, together with the elders, came up to him. "Tell us by what authority you are doing these things," they said. "Who gave you this authority?" He replied, "I will also ask you a question. Tell me: John's baptism—was it from heaven, or of human origin?"

They discussed it among themselves and said, "If we say, 'From heaven,' he will ask, 'Why didn't you believe him?' But if we say, 'Of human origin,' all the people will stone us, because they are persuaded that John was a prophet."

So they answered, "We don't know where it was from."

Jesus said, "Neither will I tell you by what authority I am doing these things."

He went on to tell the people this parable: "A man planted a vineyard, rented it to some farmers and went away for a long time. At harvest time he sent a servant to the tenants so they would give him some of the fruit of the vineyard. But the tenants beat him and sent him away empty-handed. He sent another servant, but that one also they beat and treated shamefully and sent away empty-handed. He sent still a third, and they wounded him and threw him out. Then the owner of the vineyard said, 'What shall I do? I will send my son, whom I love; perhaps they will respect him.' But when the tenants saw him, they talked the matter over. 'This is the heir,' they said. 'Let's kill him, and the inheritance will be ours.' So they threw him out of the vineyard and killed him. What then will the owner of the vineyard do to them? He will come and kill those tenants and give the vineyard to others."

When the people heard this, they said, "God forbid!"

Jesus looked directly at them and asked, "Then what is the meaning of that which is written:

"'The stone the builders rejected
has become the cornerstone'?

Everyone who falls on that stone will be broken to pieces; anyone on whom it falls will be crushed."

Consider This

Revolution begins with reform at the home office. Scan back through your Old Testament and you will see it throughout.

Whenever God wants to initiate dramatic activity in Israel's midst, he begins with their worship practices. He goes straight to the home office.

Remember the story of Gideon in the book of Judges? Here's what the angel told Gideon:

> "Take your father's bull, and the second bull seven years old, and pull down the altar of Baal that your father has, and cut down the Asherah that is beside it and build an altar to the LORD your God on the top of the stronghold here, with stones laid in due order. Then take the second bull and offer it as a burnt offering with the wood of the Asherah that you shall cut down." (Judg. 6:25–26 ESV)

How about Elijah?

> Then Elijah said to all the people, "Come near to me." And all the people came near to him. And he repaired the altar of the LORD that had been thrown down. Elijah took twelve stones, according to the number of the tribes of the sons of Jacob, to whom the word of the LORD had come, saying, "Israel shall be your name." (1 Kings 18:30–31 ESV)

Then there's Josiah's famous reform.

> And the king commanded Hilkiah the high priest and the priests of the second order and the keepers of the threshold to bring out of the temple of the Lord all the vessels made for Baal, for Asherah, and for all the host

of heaven. He burned them outside Jerusalem in the fields of the Kidron and carried their ashes to Bethel. And he deposed the priests whom the kings of Judah had ordained to make offerings in the high places at the cities of Judah and around Jerusalem; those also who burned incense to Baal, to the sun and the moon and the constellations and all the host of the heavens. And he brought out the Asherah from the house of the Lord, outside Jerusalem, to the brook Kidron, and burned it at the brook Kidron and beat it to dust and cast the dust of it upon the graves of the common people. (2 Kings 23:4–6 ESV)

When God is going to make a move, he begins by restoring the center of worship. Jesus is neither a Pharisee nor a scribe nor a priest nor a religious leader, but he heads straight to the center of worship, the symbolic center of the universe: the temple. He's about to turn everything around.

"It is written," he said to them, "'My house will be a house of prayer'; but you have made it 'a den of robbers.'"

Interestingly, the temple should have been a place where the poor and the oppressed found refuge. Instead, they found themselves pushed to the very margins of the society. They had been robbed of their place in the presence of God. God intended the temple to be a place of centrifugal blessing—spinning outward the grace and mercy of God. The religious establishment had turned it into a place of centripetal privilege—pulling inward worldly status, wealth, and privilege. The exact opposite of what God intended had happened.

Jesus, the one greater than the temple, turns it inside out and upside down in his mission to turn everything around.

Soon Jerusalem will be the place from which the Word goes out, a place of sending, where the gospel moves outward with the Holy Spirit's centrifugal power of love to Judea, Samaria, and away to the ends of the earth.

For too long now, the church has been a centripetal institution, a place of elaborate edifices where power and privilege and wealth collect. No wonder we speak so much of going to church. Once again, the poor and the oppressed find themselves pushed out to the margins of society and blamed for their own condition. Is it time for some reform at the home office again?

Holy Week is upon us, but we must decide. Will it be another trip through the ritualistic ruts of our religious track—a parade of pomp and circumstance? Or will we invite Jesus to come in and turn over some tables, maybe institute a little apostolic reform, or a lot?

The Prayer

Lord Jesus Christ, Son of God, have mercy on me, a sinner.
Lord Jesus Christ, Son of God, have mercy on me, a
    son/daughter.
Lord Jesus Christ, Son of God, have mercy on me, a saint.

The Question

How will Holy Week be different for you this year—more than just another lap around the religious track?

Sixth Sunday of Lent

Start Caring More

LUKE 20:19–47 | The teachers of the law and the chief priests looked for a way to arrest him immediately, because they knew he had spoken this parable against them. But they were afraid of the people.

Keeping a close watch on him, they sent spies, who pretended to be sincere. They hoped to catch Jesus in something he said, so that they might hand him over to the power and authority of the governor. So the spies questioned him: "Teacher, we know that you speak and teach what is right, and that you do not show partiality but teach the way of God in accordance with the truth. Is it right for us to pay taxes to Caesar or not?"

He saw through their duplicity and said to them, "Show me a denarius. Whose image and inscription are on it?"

"Caesar's," they replied.

He said to them, "Then give back to Caesar what is Caesar's, and to God what is God's."

They were unable to trap him in what he had said there in public. And astonished by his answer, they became silent.

Some of the Sadducees, who say there is no resurrection, came to Jesus with a question. "Teacher," they said, "Moses wrote for us that if a man's brother dies and leaves a wife but no children, the man must marry the widow and raise up offspring for his brother. Now there were seven brothers. The first one married a woman and died childless. The second and then the third married her, and in the same way the seven died, leaving no children. Finally, the woman died too. Now then, at the resurrection whose wife will she be, since the seven were married to her?"

Jesus replied, "The people of this age marry and are given in marriage. But those who are considered worthy of taking part in the age to come and in the resurrection from the dead will neither marry nor be given in marriage, and they can no longer die; for they are like the angels. They are God's children, since they are children of the resurrection. But in the account of the burning bush, even Moses showed that the dead rise, for he calls the Lord 'the God of Abraham, and the God of Isaac, and the God of Jacob.' He is not the God of the dead, but of the living, for to him all are alive."

Some of the teachers of the law responded, "Well said, teacher!" And no one dared to ask him any more questions.

Then Jesus said to them, "Why is it said that the Messiah is the son of David? David himself declares in the Book of Psalms:

"'The Lord said to my Lord:
"Sit at my right hand
until I make your enemies
a footstool for your feet."'

David calls him 'Lord.' How then can he be his son?"

While all the people were listening, Jesus said to his disciples, "Beware of the teachers of the law. They like to walk around in flowing robes and love to be greeted with respect in the marketplaces and have the most important seats in the synagogues and the places of honor at banquets. They devour widows' houses and for a show make lengthy prayers. These men will be punished most severely."

Consider This

The definitive sign that people are worshipping the one true and living God is seen in the way they care for the least among them. The definitive sign of idolatry, that people are worshipping a false God, is seen in the way the so-called people of God can turn a blind eye to those in need.

Jesus, the Son of God, the God for whom the temple was built, the One who is greater than the temple, now stands in the midst of it. The television show *Undercover Boss* comes to mind.

In this case, he finds the place sieged by rogue religious leaders. It's like a conspiracy of employees trying to throw him out by throwing the policy manual at him. They actually stoop to a thinly veiled defense of Caesar. I mean, Jesus would never stick it to Rome, would he? That would destroy our way of life. And those Sadducees with their ridiculous question about this seventh marriage issue. It's another cheaply cloaked attempt to get him to contradict Moses. Finally, as if to say, "That's all you've got?" Jesus pitches them a messianic riddle of his own.

After this tiresome exercise in missing the point, he delivers the zinger, illustrating the absurdity of all they had come to spend their time focusing on.

"They like to walk around in flowing robes and love to be greeted with respect in the marketplaces and have the most important seats in the synagogues and the places of honor at banquets. They devour widows' houses and for a show make lengthy prayers. These men will be punished most severely."

And if I'm honest, I must confess my own resemblance to such an excoriating characterization. I'm not too big on the robe idea, but I do like to be greeted with respect in the marketplace. I like the front row seats, and I love to be given a place of honor at important occasions. I like to know and be known by important people, and I like others to know it. And that's where I would like to draw the line—which is the problem. I just don't see myself devouring widows' houses. We never do. Here's how that works. It's not that we actively devour widows' houses so much as we make worship (and church) all about feeding our own appetites and needs. This explains how I can ignore a man holding a "Will work for food" sign on my way to church, thinking to myself something like, *This guy probably has a BMW parked across town and he's just scamming us. Get a job!* Or worse, *He will probably just go buy liquor with the money.*

Church ever so subtly switches gears from the service of God to maintaining the status of its leaders and leading citizens. Nobody sets out to ignore the poor. We just get caught up in all it takes to maintain our own way of life. Before we know it, we've gotten God all caught up in all it takes to maintain our way of life. That's how it happens.

And this isn't a problem more charity can solve. It will take a genuine revolution of caring. At least I think that's what Jesus cares about.

The Prayer

Lord Jesus Christ, Son of God, have mercy on me, a sinner.
Lord Jesus Christ, Son of God, have mercy on me, a
   son/daughter.
Lord Jesus Christ, Son of God, have mercy on me, a saint.

The Question

Devouring widows' houses? Can you see it? Do two copper coins ring a bell? It will.

My Two Cents' Worth? 35

LUKE 21:1–4 ESV | Jesus looked up and saw the rich putting their gifts into the offering box, and he saw a poor widow put in two small copper coins. And he said, "Truly I tell you, this poor widow has put in more than all of them. For they all contributed out of their abundance, but she out of her poverty put in all she had to live on."

Consider This

Friends, the texts are going to get longer this week, and because of the gravity of these Holy Week texts (in comparison to what I have to say about them), I am going to shorten my comments. By the time we get to Thursday I may have nothing to say at all. Nothing is more critical this week than the slow, deliberate, even contemplative reading of these texts.

Think about it—apart from these written gospel accounts, we would know nothing at all about Jesus. This is a week to treasure the text. I encourage you to read it aloud so your ears can physically hear the words. Faith, remember, comes by hearing.

Now to my short comment for the day: I always understood the story about the widow putting all she had to live on in the temple treasury as a good thing—a commendation of the widow. When I look again and read it carefully in its context, I am beginning to think it was actually a bad thing.

The reality is that it was an indictment on the temple and its leadership—remember that word about devouring the houses of widows? It's easy for a wealthy community leader to put in a fraction of a fraction of their wealth into the offering plate while having no idea that it costs the most impoverished among them everything they have to even participate. It gets really interesting when on the heels of this story, Jesus' disciples start pointing out the extravagance of the temple.

I mean, would that be what Jesus is really after—for the poor to take what little they have and put it into the offering plate? Surely not. Am I missing something here?

So that was the first paragraph in today's reading. The kicker comes in the rest of the story, on which I will not elaborate other than to say it's all about judgment. Are you seeing the connection?

The Prayer

Lord Jesus Christ, Son of God, have mercy on me, a sinner.
Lord Jesus Christ, Son of God, have mercy on me, a
*   son/daughter.*
Lord Jesus Christ, Son of God, have mercy on me, a saint.

The Question

Where do you most struggle with the prevailing value system within the church in our time?

Above All, Treasure the Words of Jesus

LUKE 21:5–36 | Some of his disciples were remarking about how the temple was adorned with beautiful stones and with gifts dedicated to God. But Jesus said, "As for what you see here, the time will come when not one stone will be left on another; every one of them will be thrown down."

"Teacher," they asked, "when will these things happen? And what will be the sign that they are about to take place?"

He replied: "Watch out that you are not deceived. For many will come in my name, claiming, 'I am he,' and, 'The time is near.' Do not follow them. When you hear of wars and uprisings, do not be frightened. These things must happen first, but the end will not come right away."

Then he said to them: "Nation will rise against nation, and kingdom against kingdom. There will be great earthquakes, famines and pestilences in various places, and fearful events and great signs from heaven.

"But before all this, they will seize you and persecute you. They will hand you over to synagogues and put you in prison, and you will be brought before kings and governors, and all on account of my name. And so you will bear testimony to me. But make up your mind not to worry beforehand how you will defend yourselves. For I will give you words and wisdom that none of your adversaries will be able to resist or contradict. You will be betrayed even by parents, brothers and sisters, relatives and friends, and they will put some of you to death. Everyone will hate you because of me. But not a hair of your head will perish. Stand firm, and you will win life.

"When you see Jerusalem being surrounded by armies, you will know that its desolation is near. Then let those who are in Judea flee to the mountains, let those in the city get out, and let those in the country not enter the city. For this is the time of punishment in fulfillment of all that has been written. How dreadful it will be in those days for pregnant women and nursing mothers! There will be great distress in the land and wrath against this people. They will fall by the sword and will be taken as prisoners to all the nations. Jerusalem will be trampled on by the Gentiles until the times of the Gentiles are fulfilled.

"There will be signs in the sun, moon and stars. On the earth, nations will be in anguish and perplexity at the roaring and tossing of the sea. People will faint from terror, apprehensive of what is coming on the world, for the heavenly bodies will be shaken. At that time they will see the Son of Man coming in a cloud with power and great glory. When these things begin to take place, stand up and lift up your heads, because your redemption is drawing near."

He told them this parable: "Look at the fig tree and all the trees. When they sprout leaves, you can see for yourselves and know that summer is near. Even so, when you see these things happening, you know that the kingdom of God is near.

"Truly I tell you, this generation will certainly not pass away until all these things have happened. Heaven and earth will pass away, but my words will never pass away.

"Be careful, or your hearts will be weighed down with carousing, drunkenness and the anxieties of life, and that day will close on you suddenly like a trap. For it will come on all those who live on the face of the whole earth. Be always on the watch, and pray that you may be able to escape all that is about to happen, and that you may be able to stand before the Son of Man."

Consider This

This text is as complex as it is controversial with all its prophesy of both the near-term collapse of Jerusalem and the end-of-time second coming of Jesus. There has been much written on the subject and likely a lot more to come. Jerusalem did fall in AD 70 and the temple with it. We have no idea of when the end of the age will come, other than to be assured it will come like a thief in the night.

There is a word tucked into the passage I want to lift out for our focus today. It is a word for right now.

"Heaven and earth will pass away, but my words will never pass away."

It is reminiscent of the prophecy of Isaiah: "The grass withers, the flowers fades, but the word of our God will stand forever" (Isa. 40:8 ESV).

It calls to mind the illuminating word of the psalmist: "Thy word is a lamp unto my feet, and a light unto my path" (Ps. 119:105 KJV).

These words of Jesus call to mind the delight of Jeremiah when he said: "When your words came, I ate them; they were my joy and my heart's delight, for I bear your name, Lord God Almighty" (Jer. 15:16).

As we wind our way along the descending way of the cross, we can be sure of this: *"Heaven and earth will pass away, but my words will never pass away."*

Jesus never wrote a book, yet his words hold more significance and power than all the books ever written put together.

"Heaven and earth will pass away, but my words will never pass away."

His words are true, trustworthy, and transformational. They are medicinal and miraculous.

"Heaven and earth will pass away, but my words will never pass away."

Again, the psalmist reminds us:

> More to be desired are they than gold,
>   even much fine gold;
> sweeter also than honey,
>   and drippings of the honeycomb. (Ps. 19:10 ESV)

We must, however, hearken back to the word with which we began; the one we heard from the mouth of God on the Mount of Transfiguration: "A voice came from the cloud, saying, 'This is my Son, whom I have chosen; listen to him'" (Luke 9:35).

The direction of our life will be determined by the depth of our listening to Jesus. As we approach the cross, let us labor to listen more deeply than ever before.

"Heaven and earth will pass away, but my words will never pass away."

The Prayer

Lord Jesus Christ, Son of God, have mercy on me, a sinner.
Lord Jesus Christ, Son of God, have mercy on me, a son/daughter.
Lord Jesus Christ, Son of God, have mercy on me, a saint.

The Question

What keeps you from listening at the deepest level to the words of Jesus? What will help you to this end?

37 Welcome to a Place Called Vertigo

LUKE 21:37–22:38 ESV | And every day he was teaching in the temple, but at night he went out and lodged on the mount called Olivet. And early in the morning all the people came to him in the temple to hear him.

Now the Feast of Unleavened Bread drew near, which is called the Passover. And the chief priests and the scribes were seeking how to put him to death, for they feared the people.

Then Satan entered into Judas called Iscariot, who was of the number of the twelve. He went away and conferred with the chief priests and officers how he might betray him to them And they were glad, and agreed to give him money. So he consented and sought an opportunity to betray him to them in the absence of a crowd.

Then came the day of Unleavened Bread, on which the Passover lamb had to be sacrificed. So Jesus sent Peter and John, saying, "Go and prepare the Passover for us, that we may eat it." They said to him, "Where will you have us prepare it?" He said to them, "Behold, when you have entered the city, a man carrying a jar of water will meet you. Follow him into the house that he enters and tell the master of the house, 'The Teacher says to you, Where is the guest room, where I may eat the Passover with my disciples?' And he will show you a large upper room furnished; prepare it there." And they went and found it just as he had told them, and they prepared the Passover.

And when the hour came, he reclined at table, and the apostles with him. And he said to them, "I have earnestly desired to eat this Passover with you before I suffer. For I tell you I will not eat it until it is fulfilled in the kingdom of God." And he took a cup, and when he had given thanks he said, "Take this, and divide it among yourselves. For I tell you that from now on I will not drink of the fruit of the vine until the kingdom of God comes." And he took bread, and when he had given thanks, he broke it and gave it to them, saying, "This is my body, which is given for you. Do this in remembrance of me." And likewise the cup after they had eaten, saying, "This cup that is poured out for you is the new covenant in my blood. But behold, the hand of him who betrays me is with me on the table. For the Son of Man goes as it has been determined, but woe to that man by whom he is betrayed!" And they began to question one another, which of them it could be who was going to do this.

A dispute also arose among them, as to which of them was to be regarded as the greatest. And he said to them, "The kings of the Gentiles exercise lordship over them, and those in authority over them are called benefactors. But not so with you. Rather, let the greatest among you become as the youngest, and the leader as one who serves. For who is the greater, one who reclines at table or one who serves? Is it not the one who reclines at table? But I am among you as the one who serves.

"You are those who have stayed with me in my trials, and I assign to you, as my Father assigned to me, a kingdom, that you may eat and drink at my table in my kingdom and sit on thrones judging the twelve tribes of Israel.

"Simon, Simon, behold, Satan demanded to have you, that he might sift you like wheat, but I have prayed for you that your faith may not fail. And when you have turned again, strengthen your brothers. Peter said to him, "Lord, I am ready to go with you both to prison and to death." Jesus said, "I tell you, Peter, the rooster will not crow this day, until you deny three times that you know me."

And he said to them, "When I sent you out with no moneybag or knapsack or sandals, did you lack anything?" They said, "Nothing." He said to them, "But now let the one who has a moneybag take it, and likewise a knapsack. And let the one who has no sword sell his cloak and buy one. For I tell you that this Scripture must be fulfilled in me: 'And he was numbered with the transgressors.' For what is written about me has its fulfillment." And they said, "Look, Lord, here are two swords." And he said to them, "It is enough."

Consider This

The Passion is upon us. As promised, since these readings are significant in length, I will keep my comments brief.

What I want you to pay particular attention to over these next few days are the surprising and terribly unlikely responses of the cast of characters and the stunning reversals of reality.

Judas, the disciple of Jesus, breaks ranks and betrays him. Joseph of Arimathea, an elite Pharisee, breaks ranks and buries him. Peter, his chief disciple, disowns him. His chief executioner, a Roman centurion, extols him. A Roman governor tries to release him. An unnamed criminal places faith in him.

Things couldn't be more confusing. In the chaos of the Creator's crucifixion comes the stunning revelation of who stands with who. Upside down is right side up now. Least is greatest. Last is first. High noon will become pitch dark. In remembering the ancient history of the Passover, the door to the eternal kingdom of God opens wide.

This is April Fool's Day on steroids—only it's no joke. So it is with the foolishness of the cross. "For the foolishness of God is wiser than men, and the weakness of God is stronger than men" (1 Cor. 1:25 ESV).

Kneeling . . . it's the only way to stand in a week like this. It's why we need the prayer more than ever . . .

The Prayer

Lord Jesus Christ, Son of God, have mercy on me, a sinner.
Lord Jesus Christ, Son of God, have mercy on me, a
*   son/daughter.*
Lord Jesus Christ, Son of God, have mercy on me, a saint.

The Question

Where and how do you see the foolishness of the cross afoot in your life just now? In your past? Your future?

38 Maundy Thursday

In solemn remembrance of the events of Holy Week, I have elected to forgo any of my comments so that full attention can be given to the Word of God. Please read slowly, deliberately, reverently, and aloud.

LUKE 22:39–65 THE MESSAGE | Leaving there, he went, as he so often did, to Mount Olives. The disciples followed him. When they arrived at the place, he said, "Pray that you don't give in to temptation."

He pulled away from them about a stone's throw, knelt down, and prayed, "Father, remove this cup from me. But please, not what I want. What do you want?" At once an angel from heaven was at his side, strengthening him. He prayed on all the harder. Sweat, wrung from him like drops of blood, poured off his face.

He got up from prayer, went back to the disciples and found them asleep, drugged by grief. He said, "What business do you have sleeping? Get up. Pray so you won't give in to temptation."

No sooner were the words out of his mouth than a crowd showed up, Judas, the one from the Twelve, in the lead. He came right up to Jesus to kiss him. Jesus said, "Judas, you would betray the Son of Man with a kiss?"

When those with him saw what was happening, they said, "Master, shall we fight?" One of them took a swing at the Chief Priest's servant and cut off his right ear.

Jesus said, "Let them be. Even in this." Then, touching the servant's ear, he healed him.

Jesus spoke to those who had come—high priests, Temple police, religion leaders: "What is this, jumping me with swords and clubs as if I were a dangerous criminal? Day after day I've been with you in the Temple and you've not so much as lifted a hand against me. But do it your way—it's a dark night, a dark hour."

Arresting Jesus, they marched him off and took him into the house of the Chief Priest. Peter followed, but at a safe distance. In the middle of the courtyard some people had started a fire and were sitting around it, trying to keep warm. One of the serving maids sitting at the fire noticed him, then took a second look and said, "This man was with him!"

He denied it, "Woman, I don't even know him."

A short time later, someone else noticed him and said, "You're one of them."

But Peter denied it: "Man, I am not."

About an hour later, someone else spoke up, really adamant: "He's got to have been with him! He's got 'Galilean' written all over him."

Peter said, "Man, I don't know what you're talking about." At that very moment, the last word hardly off his lips, a rooster crowed. Just then, the Master turned and looked at Peter. Peter remembered what the Master had said to him: "Before the rooster crows, you will deny me three times." He went out and cried and cried and cried.

The men in charge of Jesus began poking fun at him, slapping him around. They put a blindfold on him and taunted, "Who hit you that time?" They were having a grand time with him.

The Prayer

Lord Jesus Christ, Son of God, have mercy on me, a sinner.
Lord Jesus Christ, Son of God, have mercy on me, a son/daughter.
Lord Jesus Christ, Son of God, have mercy on me, a saint.

The Question

Were you there when they crucified my Lord?

39 Good Friday

In solemn remembrance of the events of Holy Week, I have elected to forgo any of my comments so that full attention can be given to the Word of God. Please read slowly, deliberately, reverently, and aloud.

LUKE 22:66–23:49 THE MESSAGE | When it was morning, the religious leaders of the people and the high priests and scholars all got together and brought him before their High Council. They said, "Are you the Messiah?"

He answered, "If I said yes, you wouldn't believe me. If I asked what you meant by your question, you wouldn't answer me. So here's what I have to say: From here on the Son of Man takes his place at God's right hand, the place of power."

They all said, "So you admit your claim to be the Son of God?"

"You're the ones who keep saying it," he said.

But they had made up their minds, "Why do we need any more evidence? We've all heard him as good as say it himself."

Then they all took Jesus to Pilate and began to bring up charges against him. They said, "We found this man undermining our law and order, forbidding taxes to be paid to Caesar, setting himself up as Messiah–King."

Pilate asked him, "Is this true that you're 'King of the Jews'?"

"Those are your words, not mine," Jesus replied.

Pilate told the high priests and the accompanying crowd, "I find nothing wrong here. He seems harmless enough to me."

But they were vehement. "He's stirring up unrest among the people with his teaching, disturbing the peace everywhere, starting in Galilee and now all through Judea. He's a dangerous man, endangering the peace."

When Pilate heard that, he asked, "So, he's a Galilean?" Realizing that he properly came under Herod's jurisdiction, he passed the buck to Herod, who just happened to be in Jerusalem for a few days.

Herod was delighted when Jesus showed up. He had wanted for a long time to see him, he'd heard so much about him. He hoped to see him do something spectacular. He peppered him with questions. Jesus didn't answer—not one word. But the high priests and religion scholars were right there, saying their piece, strident and shrill in their accusations.

Mightily offended, Herod turned on Jesus. His soldiers joined in, taunting and jeering. Then they dressed him up in an elaborate king costume and sent him back to Pilate. That day Herod and Pilate became thick as thieves. Always before they had kept their distance.

Then Pilate called in the high priests, rulers, and the others and said, "You brought this man to me as a disturber of the peace. I examined him in front of all of you and found there was nothing to your charge. And neither did Herod, for he has sent him back here with a clean bill of health. It's clear that he's done nothing wrong, let alone anything deserving death. I'm going to warn him to watch his step and let him go."

At that, the crowd went wild: "Kill him! Give us Barabbas!" (Barabbas had been thrown in prison for starting a riot in the city and for murder.) Pilate still wanted to let Jesus go, and so spoke out again.

But they kept shouting back, "Crucify! Crucify him!"

He tried a third time. "But for what crime? I've found nothing in him deserving death. I'm going to warn him to watch his step and let him go."

But they kept at it, a shouting mob, demanding that he be crucified. And finally they shouted him down. Pilate caved in and gave them what they wanted. He released the man thrown in prison for rioting and murder, and gave them Jesus to do whatever they wanted.

As they led him off, they made Simon, a man from Cyrene who happened to be coming in from the countryside, carry the cross behind Jesus. A huge crowd of people followed, along with women weeping and carrying on. At one point Jesus turned to the women and said, "Daughters of Jerusalem, don't cry for me. Cry for yourselves and for your children. The time is coming when they'll say, 'Lucky the women who never conceived! Lucky the wombs that never gave birth! Lucky the breasts that never gave milk!' Then they'll start calling to the mountains, 'Fall down on us!' calling to the hills, 'Cover us up!' If people do these things to a live, green tree, can you imagine what they'll do with deadwood?"

Two others, both criminals, were taken along with him for execution.

When they got to the place called Skull Hill, they crucified him, along with the criminals, one on his right, the other on his left.

Jesus prayed, "Father, forgive them; they don't know what they're doing."

Dividing up his clothes, they threw dice for them. The people stood there staring at Jesus, and the ringleaders made faces, taunting, "He saved others. Let's see him save himself! The Messiah of God—ha! The Chosen—ha!"

The soldiers also came up and poked fun at him, making a game of it. They toasted him with sour wine: "So you're King of the Jews! Save yourself!"

Printed over him was a sign: THIS IS THE KING OF THE JEWS.

One of the criminals hanging alongside cursed him: "Some Messiah you are! Save yourself! Save us!"

But the other one made him shut up: "Have you no fear of God? You're getting the same as him. We deserve this, but not him— he did nothing to deserve this."

Then he said, "Jesus, remember me when you enter your kingdom."

He said, "Don't worry, I will. Today you will join me in paradise."

By now it was noon. The whole earth became dark, the darkness lasting three hours—a total blackout. The Temple curtain split right down the middle. Jesus called loudly, "Father, I place my life in your hands!" Then he breathed his last.

When the captain there saw what happened, he honored God: "This man was innocent! A good man, and innocent!"

All who had come around as spectators to watch the show, when they saw what actually happened, were overcome with grief and headed home. Those who knew Jesus well, along with the women who had followed him from Galilee, stood at a respectful distance and kept vigil.

The Prayer

Lord Jesus Christ, Son of God, have mercy on me, a sinner.
Lord Jesus Christ, Son of God, have mercy on me, a
son/daughter.
Lord Jesus Christ, Son of God, have mercy on me, a saint.

The Question

Were you there when they nailed him to the tree?

Holy Saturday

40

In solemn remembrance of the events of Holy Week, I have elected to forgo any of my comments so that full attention can be given to the Word of God. Please read slowly, deliberately, reverently, and aloud.

LUKE 23:50–56 THE MESSAGE | There was a man by the name of Joseph, a member of the Jewish High Council, a man of good heart and good character. He had not gone along with the plans and actions of the council. His hometown was the Jewish village of Arimathea. He lived in alert expectation of the kingdom of God. He went to Pilate and asked for the body of Jesus. Taking him down, he wrapped him in a linen shroud and placed him in a tomb chiseled into the rock, a tomb never yet used. It was the day before Sabbath, the Sabbath just about to begin.

The women who had been companions of Jesus from Galilee followed along. They saw the tomb where Jesus' body was placed. Then they went back to prepare burial spices and perfumes. They rested quietly on the Sabbath, as commanded.

The Prayer
Lord Jesus Christ, Son of God, have mercy on me, a sinner.
Lord Jesus Christ, Son of God, have mercy on me, a
*   son/daughter.*
Lord Jesus Christ, Son of God, have mercy on me, a saint.

The Question
Were you there when they laid him in the tomb?

Easter Sunday

HE IS RISEN!

LUKE 24:1–8 THE MESSAGE | At the crack of dawn on Sunday, the women came to the tomb carrying the burial spices they had prepared. They found the entrance stone rolled back from the tomb, so they walked in. But once inside, they couldn't find the body of the Master Jesus.

They were puzzled, wondering what to make of this. Then, out of nowhere it seemed, two men, light cascading over them, stood there. The women were awestruck and bowed down in worship. The men said, "Why are you looking for the Living One in a cemetery? He is not here, but raised up. Remember how he told you when you were still back in Galilee that he had to be handed over to sinners, be killed on a cross, and in three days rise up?" Then they remembered Jesus' words.

HE IS RISEN INDEED!

Appendix A
The Nine Prayers of Jesus

1. "Our Father in heaven . . ." (Matt. 6:9–13).
2. "I thank you, Father, Lord of heaven and earth, that you have hidden these things from the wise and understanding and revealed them to little children; yes, Father, for such was your gracious will" (Matt. 11:25–26 ESV).
3. "Father, I thank you that you have heard me. I knew that you always hear me, but I said this for the benefit of the people standing here, that they may believe that you sent me. . . . Lazarus, come out!" (John 11:41–43).
4. "Now my soul is troubled, and what shall I say? 'Father, save me from this hour'? No, it was for this very reason I came to this hour. Abba, glorify your name!" (John 12:27–28).
5. "Abba, Father, everything is possible for you. Take this cup from me. Yet not what I will, but what you will" (Mark 14:36).
6. "Father, forgive them, for they do not know what they are doing" (Luke 23:34).
7. "'Eloi, Eloi, lama sabachthani?' (which means 'My God, my God, why have you forsaken me?')" (Mark 15:34).
8. "Father, into your hands I commit my spirit" (Luke 23:46).

9. "My prayer is not for them alone. I pray also for those who will believe in me through their message, that all of them may be one, Father, just as you are in me and I am in you. May they also be in us so that the world may believe that you have sent me. . . ." (John 17:1–26).

Appendix B
THE SOWER'S CREED

Today I sow, for a great awakening.

Today, I stake everything on the promise of the Word of God. I depend entirely on the power of the Holy Spirit. I have the same mind in me that was in Christ Jesus. Because Jesus is good news and Jesus is in me, I am good news.

Today, I will sow the extravagance of the gospel everywhere I go and into everyone I meet.

Today, I will love others as Jesus has loved me.

Today, I will remember that the tiniest seeds become the tallest trees; that the seeds sown today become the shade of tomorrow; that the faith of right now becomes the future of the everlasting kingdom.

Today, I sow for a great awakening.